ANCIENT

A study of the archaeology
and prehistory of Exmoor.

Hazel Eardley-Wilmot

The Exmoor Press

★

MICROSTUDIES

Each Microstudy has been written by an expert and is designed to appeal to all who are interested in Exmoor.

The Editor of the Series is Victor Bonham-Carter.

A list of all the titles is available from

The Exmoor Press   Dulverton   Somerset

★

Printed by The Furnival Press, London

Contents

Illustrations

Photographs
The British Museum (by permission of the Trustees), p.44; S. H. Burton, p.72 and back cover; Michael Deering, pp.10, 67; Ivan Durman, p.4; Arthur Phillips, pp.16, 26, 30, 38, 39, 46, 47, 59; John Pedder, p.22; Charles Whybrow, pp.17, 49, 54, 64.

Drawing
Audrey Wilson, p.69.

Maps
The map of prehistoric sites on pp.36-7, and the diagram on p.62 have been devised by the author from the Ordnance Survey 1 inch map of Exmoor, and given final form by Norma Deering—by permission of the Controller of Her Majesty's Stationery Office, Crown copyright reserved.

Front Cover   *Back Cover*
The Wheeled Cross Stone, Culbone   Longstone Barrow

The Author

Hazel Eardley-Wilmot, an Oxford graduate in English, does not claim to be more than a serious amateur in archaeology, but she brings to the study of Exmoor's prehistory a variety of experience in other professions, both in England and abroad, some acquaintance with the vagaries of language, and in one way and another nearly fifty years of gradually becoming familiar with the moor.

Since finding White Ladder in 1975 she has investigated a number of unrecorded monuments and written about some of them in Devon and Somerset periodicals and the *Exmoor Review*. She believes that careful noticing and unhurried thinking may enable almost anyone to add to the slender total of knowledge about Exmoor's remote past.

Heddon Stone.

Introduction

So many 'new' ancient sites have been recognised on Exmoor in the last few years that Charles Whybrow's *Antiquary's Exmoor,* that good sound little book first published by the Exmoor Press in 1970, now needs a sequel rather than a fresh edition. In revising it himself for the second edition in 1977, the year before he died, he added further information but did not recast the book. He knew his Exmoor well, had many finds and a few excavations to his credit, and had published special work on the hill forts. He was also a Fellow of the Society of Antiquaries, and watched all archaeological progress with a proper blend of generosity and scepticism. He would have been very much interested in what has been observed on the moor since his death.

The last two decades have seen far-reaching changes in archaeology everywhere—advances in factual knowledge, new scientific methods, fresh ideas, and re-appraisal of much that had seemed certain. In Britain there has been a great deal of new discovery, some of it research work, some of it 'rescue' before the construction of motorways, or urban demolition for rebuilding, or, in the country, deeper ploughing than was formerly possible.

On Exmoor, fresh knowledge is due partly to field work, and partly to the scrutiny of new air photographs, which have shown some 2000 old disturbances of the soil in about 300 square miles. Many of these are only old peat cuttings, roadmen's quarries, or vestiges of army training in the second world war, but many are much older and more interesting. When these are being checked on the ground, or when observant people merely stroll about the moor, other unrecorded traces of antiquity appear. This is happening all the time. The 'new' stone patterns or low earthworks are seldom discoveries, really. Most of them are familiar to farmers or shepherds working with livestock, and to other Exmoor people who have passed them often, on foot or on horseback, without knowing what they were. Trained archaeologists, on the other hand, are now examining them in the light of their fuller experience else-where, but without the effortless knowledge of the moor which lifelong residents can command.

Specialists and local observers are both needed. While knowledge is so fluid, perhaps a short book about material still under review may have its uses. It, too, may soon be out of date, but archaeological work is not competitive; it is a relay race against time and destruction, each investigator trying to take knowledge a little further, remove an obstacle or two, and record any lucky glimpse or surmise which may help later on.

This is neither a guide to the monuments nor a list of them. The Ordnance Survey maps, 2½ ins and 6ins, nearly all of them recently revised, place the chief known antiquities with a professional accuracy hard to emulate on Exmoor, which has few salient landmarks. Recent finds are being charted by the County Council archaeologists in Taunton and Exeter, who are glad to give or receive information. It seemed better to select some characteristic sites, outline what is known about them, and indicate possible explanations and unsolved puzzles. The emphasis is on the centuries before written history, when the ground evidence is all we have. That is very vulnerable. Small stones fall and are soon overgrown, low banks wear away. Recognition and unceasing care are needed if the shadowy record is to be preserved.

Signs of human activity during most of the six or seven thousand years from Mesolithic to Saxon times are few and scattered, but for the second and early first millennia BC—roughly, the Bronze Age—they abound. Possibly on account of the difficult climate, unbroken continuity seems to have been rare up here during prehistory, but the many barrows and banks and standing stones may be able to tell us much more than we yet know about the beliefs and life of the Bronze Age moor dwellers of some three and a half thousand years ago. These, therefore, fill the centre of this book.

★

Chapters 1 and 2 gather up different kinds of more or less common knowledge, to sketch the background. In Chapters 3 and 4 much is new since Charles Whybrow wrote, and some of it has not appeared in print until now. Chapter 5 draws freely on his study of the Iron Age and Roman forts.

Over the last seven years of fieldwork I have had invaluable help and encouragement both from trained archaeologists and from people with intimate knowledge of the moor, and I hope they all know how grateful I am. But any blunders in this book are entirely my own.

H.E-W.

1   *The Land and the Climate*

Almost anywhere on Exmoor you can see against the skyline one or more of the big round barrows where Bronze Age people buried certain of their dead. The barrows are like the Wiltshire ones near Stonehenge, and of about the same period; that means they were built about three and a half thousand years ago—before the fall of Troy, before Moses induced Pharaoh to let the Israelites leave Egypt, and long before the foundation of Rome. But neither here nor in Wiltshire were the people who made the round barrows the first inhabitants; men and women had been roaming the uplands for many thousand years before that. Some of them may have been hunting deer, spearing fish, cracking hazel nuts and sampling berries and fungi, high on Exmoor, long before the Atlantic tides, pushing up-channel, finally cut this island off from the Continent, round about 6000 BC.

The landscape was already dominated, as it is now, by three long east-west ridges. The most northerly is above the steep cliffs of the Bristol Channel—once called the Severn Sea, which may have meant 'the western sea' to very early people crossing the island by ancient trade routes. The southernmost, from Shoulsbury to East Anstey, looks across mid-Devon to Dartmoor. Along the centre is the high watershed of the Chains, the backbone of the moor. Spurs run north and south from the ridges, and the streams in deep combes between them can rise very quickly and become impassable in bad weather.

This formation had been determined 400 million years earlier, when the area of Exmoor was shallow sea, close to a northern mass of land. The rivers draining this emptied into the sea, and periodic changes of sea level produced alternate layers of red and brown sandstones and grey shales. Later earth movements raised the three long sandstone ridges, with valleys between them where the softer shales were eroded. Hard stones marked with ripples like a wet sandy beach can still be found on the hill tops, testifying to these upheavals. The same movements caused the rocks to fold and crack within the crust, and quartz was deposited in the cracks; when the soft stone weathered away, hard quartz was left in great boulders, small chunks, or tiny fragments. These shine attractively in rain or sun, and have been used as landmarks or decoration for at least four thousand years. Small veins of silver, copper and iron, and a very little alluvial gold, have been worked from time to time, but never for long.

The last time the ice cap spread southward it butted against the Exmoor coast. The hills were so near that they were covered by deep ice and snow every winter, and each summer's warmth would send half-thawed sludge, stones and topsoil slipping a little further downhill before they froze again in autumn. This left parallel ridges along the slopes, and they look deceptively like strip-lynchets, the terraces of mediaeval cultivation, but many millennia were to pass before anybody began to till the ground.

By about 5500 BC the climate was moist and warm, and trees like oak, alder, lime and elm could grow, alongside the hardy pine and hazel of earlier years. This lasted through the later Mesolithic, or Middle Stone Age, and well into the New Stone Age or Neolithic. Then early in the third millennium BC came a drier and sunnier time, which continued for some fifteen centuries, and this golden weather stimulated the Bronze Age activity which can still be traced on all the uplands of south-west England. About 1200 BC the climate began to deteriorate, and as the years went on it must have become very disagreeable indeed in the hills. It was not until the middle of the earlier Iron Age, about 200 BC, that the weather improved into the kind we still know—mist and high rainfall, salty wester-lies sweeping in from the Atlantic and stunting the trees on high ground, but quick changes to sunshine and warmth in the sheltered combes.

Neolithic and Bronze Age people cut down the natural forest partly for firewood, and for building their houses, fences and stockades against wolves or raiders, and partly to clear the land for cultivation in successive patches as the soil was exhausted. Clearance would be helped by the herding of livestock at the edges of the woodland, grazing the undergrowth so that it was easier to fell the trees, with stone axes, before the first ploughing. As the population increased, more firewood was needed, more poles and stakes and more farmland. It would be easier to clear the ridges than the steep combes or the swampy valleys, and as long as the climate remained kindly the airy hills would make the pleasantest home. When the climate worsened, families moved downhill to live, and a blanket of peat thickened on the high ground which they had cultivated and left. But it was almost certainly still grazed by sheep and cattle as well as by wild deer and ponies, and seedlings had no chance to grow into trees.

In another sense, though, it continued to be true forest for a very long time. The word 'forest' originally meant *outside* something, like Forum and foreign, thus 'outland'. From the Norman Conquest onwards this was Royal Forest, i.e. wasteland where the game was strictly preserved but the rough grazing was let to neighbouring farmers. The Crown land was sold in 1820 (by then it coincided approximately with the present parish of Exmoor or Simonsbath) but Exmoor people still speak of the Forest with a clear territorial meaning; it is 'out over', and has nothing to do with trees. The word is used in that sense throughout this book.

2 *Early Inhabitants*

Knowledge of the Middle Stone Age people on Exmoor is very shadowy, deduced only from the tiny flint arrow heads and scrapers and cutting blades found on the moor, and known to characterise Mesolithic handiwork elsewhere. The little weapons and tools seem to have been knapped from beach pebbles of flint, or from chert in the gravel washed down from the Blackdown Hills. An animal might travel a long way with an arrow head in its flesh, or a hunter far from home might lose his flint knife, so a single find is flimsy evidence, but here and there enough of these microliths have been found together to suggest a very early knapping floor, a craftsman's workshop. There was a notable one at Hawkcombe Head. The people who used these tools, to kill for food and to make the hides into some kind of protection against wind and rain, wandered over the hills without human rivals for six or seven thousand years. They may then have shared their special skill with the Neolithic strangers.

These incoming people of the New Stone Age were the builders of Avebury in Wiltshire, a splendid monument by any standard, and the long barrows known on many hills in western England and in Wales— tribal tombs like family vaults, but built above ground with huge stones and then covered with turf. They had crossed the Channel during the fifth or fourth millennium BC, and were probably descended from the early farmers of the Near East, round the Black Sea and in Asia Minor, who, as their numbers increased, had pushed up the Danube, generation by generation, and then down the Rhine to the Netherlands, whence the sea-voyage to this island cannot have been very formidable— once somebody had tried and succeeded. They were migrating, not invading, so their families would come with them. They brought live-stock and seed for crops, and they understood ploughing and pottery. They had no metal, but used stone, polished for axes or rough for querns, and were well able to fell trees and shape the wood. They hunted some of their food—fishing and wild-fowling, as well as shooting with flint-headed arrows, and presumably setting snares. They also grew some corn, and kept cattle and sheep and pigs. On the Wiltshire Downs, on Sedgemoor and on Dartmoor, they used a wide range of farm-ing skills. There is no unquestionable evidence yet that they settled on Exmoor, although a knapping-floor on Kentisbury Down shows that they were here in some seasons, at least. No long barrow has yet been found, but an impressive round one on Easter New Moor, the biggest of a group along the high ridge between Molland and Knowstone, may

*WORK OF NATURE. This piece of light tawny sandstone, found in a tributary
of Farley Water, looks like a Neolithic saddle-quern not yet properly smoothed,
but geologists explain it as the result of natural mechanical processes. A Neolithic grinder
would welcome such a stone, to lessen his labour. Its effective length is 27.5 cm.,
and the hollow, like a shallow dish, is 18 cm. long.*

*WORK OF MAN. Hollowed like a cup, from a piece of very hard
dark sandstone, 16.5 cm. long. A slight overhanging rim at one end
of the oval cup shows it to have been man-made, and the pattern on the surrounding
band seems laboriously pecked. It was found by the farmer, John Milton,
near what may have been the entrance to a passage-grave on Easter New Moor.*

have been a Neolithic passage-grave, and if so, others too may be older than we have supposed. And an earthen ring on Woolhanger farm near Parracombe is believed to have been a Neolithic henge, a place of assembly and worship like the much larger ones at Marden in Wiltshire and near Priddy on Mendip.

★

During the third millennium BC new strangers began to arrive from the Continent—perhaps only a few boatloads at a time, perhaps more. There was plenty of room on the island. Other tribes followed, settled, and spread their new ideas and practical knowledge among the Neolithic farmers. The changes are evident in different styles of pottery, in different funeral customs and shapes of burial mound, and in a very important innovation—the working of metal. First copper was used alone, then tin was added to make the bronze from which the whole period is named. Perhaps Exmoor copper and Cornish tin attracted bronze-smiths and traders to the south-west. But meanwhile older customs were not abandoned. Stone and flint still made good strong tools. Ideas mingled. A chieftain might lie buried full length, Neolithic fashion, in a round barrow of Bronze Age type, and the stone circles of Dartmoor, Exmoor and Cornwall resemble the Neolithic henges. The impression is one of peaceful penetration and undisturbed development. Traces of prehistoric farming on Exmoor, not yet securely dated, may, here as on Dartmoor, overlie others in an already traditional pattern. We seem to have the ruins of a few Bronze Age houses, with circular stone footings, and entrance gaps away from the wettest and the coldest winds; probably many others were built of wood, long since rotted away.

Specialisation must have been increasing. Already there were the hunters and woodcutters and farmers, and their wives-of-all-work who ground the corn, cooked, spun, wove, and looked after the children. Perhaps pottery was becoming a full-time job. Certainly the bronze-smith was a skilled craftsman, either making fine objects at home, or travelling with tools and metal, to make or mend as required. Trade routes were impressively long. First flint and stone, now bronze and gold and jewellery as well, were used far from their places of origin. Amber from the North Sea or the Baltic formed the central bead of a necklace found in a grave at North Molton, and, studded with tiny gold pins, made the pommel of a dagger buried in a tomb on Farway Down in South Devon. The gold cup from Rillaton in Cornwall is very much like one found in a shaft-grave at Mycenae, Agamemnon's palace in southern Greece. The Neolithic monuments had implied the power to organise vast enterprises:

so now did the later versions of Stonehenge, described by an early Greek traveller as a magnificent sacred precinct and astronomical temple to the sun-god Apollo. Similarly the golden weapons and adornments buried in the great Wiltshire tombs testify to a hierarchy, and so do the impressive skyline barrows on Exmoor, robbed long ago. It looks like the Homeric world. But there does not seem to have been much war between tribes.

★

The Celts altered that. These flamboyant invaders had the great advantage of iron weapons, hitherto unknown. Iron was not only stronger than bronze but much cheaper, so the common soldier could be armed, as well as the warrior prince and his bodyguard. Resistance would be almost impossible. The first to arrive, about 500 BC, seem to have been peaceful craftsmen who mingled easily with their hosts, but the Gauls who followed were warlike aggressors. After conquering the natives they readily turned upon each other. In due course they fortified big strongholds such as Maiden Castle in Dorset, but some of the smaller hill forts may have been built against their attacks.

These barbarians were objects of curiosity to travellers from the civilised world of the Mediterranean, who recorded what they saw. The clearest report is Julius Caesar's. He found out all he could about the islanders, as a good invading general should, and set it down in *De Bello Gallico* as dispassionately as could be expected. He said that the Celts, whom the Romans counted as Gaullish, did not call themselves so, but he describes the customs of the Gauls in general, and among them the Belgae of the north-east, close kin to the immigrant tribes he encountered along the British coast. He found them brave fighters and clever tacticians, but treacherous, and endlessly divided among themselves.

In Gaul, he said, there were two ruling castes, the priests, or druids, and the knights; the rest were treated almost as slaves. The druids, highly privileged, conducted all religious and most legal matters, and they educated young men orally in their own doctrines, which under strict taboo were not to be put in writing. But the early Iron Age Gauls were not illiterate; they used the Greek alphabet for keeping their financial accounts. Their gods were very much like those of the Mediterranean; but the Gauls were, Caesar records, extremely superstitious, and the druids conducted particularly horrible and wholesale state sacrifices with their fellow tribesmen as victims.

In his expedition to Britain in 55 BC Caesar found that the lands along the south coast, which the Gauls held, were thickly studded with homesteads; corn, cattle and timber were plentiful, and he gives an attractive domestic detail; although they thought it unlawful to eat hares, fowl or geese, they reared them for pleasure and amusement. But battle was a sterner sport. Interrupted in the middle of corn harvest by the approach of nearly a hundred Roman ships bristling with soldiers, they mustered quickly with horses and chariots and javelins, and made the landing very difficult indeed. Neither Caesar's short campaign that year nor his longer one the following summer was an unqualified success, and it was nearly a century before Rome tried again.

Caesar's report is about people. The evidence from the ground is more limited. It consists chiefly of the hill forts, or 'castles', and the elaborate 'Celtic' decorative art. Some of this was panoply of war, but some was graceful and delicate, like the Holcombe mirror from South Devon. The only Exmoor example yet found is a bronze bowl from Munson farm, Rose Ash, and this is now in the British Museum. The hill forts are plentiful, though their purpose is not always clear. For lack of excavation and dating we do not really know who was frightened of whom, nor whether the strong ramparts were for domination or refuge. There must in any case have been a great difference between the life of the hill people, struggling for subsistence in miserable weather, and that of the swashbuckling raiders further down. No wonder that so few traces except the hill forts remain; but there may be clues to understanding still buried in the ground.

★

The Roman invasion of AD 43 brought the island gradually into the civilised world, and also out of prehistory into the written record for a time. Archaeologists unearth supplementary detail of the conquest, the military occupation, the increasingly comfortable colonial life for 'Roman citizens' (of any nationality) in the south, and the unending friction on the northern borders. Most of Britain was a Roman colony for nearly four centuries, but during the last of these the frontiers of the empire were slowly crumbling, and in 410 AD the legions were recalled to Italy to protect Rome itself from barbarian hordes. Then the British had to defend themselves as best they could.

Little of all this touched Exmoor, so far as we know. There were two small forts or signal stations on the north coast, at Old Burrow and Martinhoe, manned to keep watch against the untamed Silures of South Wales, but the conqueror's network of roads and forts seems to have passed east, west and south of the misty hills, not across them. If the purpose was quick travel to and from Exeter, that made very good sense.

13

During the fifth and sixth centuries, with the lights going out all over Europe, the Romanised Britons kept a little candle burning for a while. Vigorous pagan Angles and Saxons were conquering the lowlands with ease, but west of Wansdyke the British held out under their commander-in-chief, Arthur, later thought of nostalgically as *Rex quondam Rexque futurus,* the former king who would return. South Cadbury hill fort, above the river Cam, near Roman Ilchester and some twelve miles south-east of Glastonbury, may have been re-used as a stronghold in this resistance. It was probably Arthur who defeated the Saxons in a famous battle, which deterred them for half-a-century. But old history was repeated; as Caesar and then Tacitus had remarked, the Celtic tribes could not hold together for long. Arthur's own armies quarrelled. In essence it was the tragedy in which Malory's great book culminated, nearly a thousand years later—bitter strife among kinsmen causing irreparable ruin.

Perhaps at first Exmoor people would see little change, and as former Roman citizens they may for a time have felt more Roman than ever before. The Caratacus inscription on a small longstone on Winsford hill is in fifth or sixth century Latin lettering, not in the Celtic alphabet, Ogam; so is the one near Lynton commemorating Cavudus. The Romans had imported Christianity to the towns, towards the end of their tenure. Now Irish and Welsh missionaries came in across the Severn Sea, and the coastwise churches and villages named after these holy men—Petrock at Parracombe, Beuno at Culbone, Brendan at Brendon—recall the centuries between Roman and Saxon rule. By the time the English came to Exmoor in the eighth century, tramping in from Taunton along the prehistoric ridgeway which they renamed Herepath, the army road, they were Christian invaders of a Christian country, and there is no evidence of serious clashes. But we do not know, and perhaps never shall. The Dark Ages were murky times to live in, and are now well-nigh impenetrably obscure.

With the arrival of the Saxons we are almost home. We speak their language, and live in villages once theirs. We have the historical records begun at Winchester by the great humane English king, Alfred. Above all, we have their poetry, telling directly what they thought and felt about life. These are not strangers.

They were part of the new civilisation, Christendom, which was slowly taking shape. As they settled in the valleys, ancient Exmoor began to be hidden in the hill mists.

14

3   Barrows and Stones

When one tries to read the ground of Exmoor itself, to see what was happening at any particular time, there is very little to be sure of. The scattered bits of evidence must signify something, but they are like pieces of half-a-dozen jigsaw puzzles all jumbled together, with nothing to show which scrap belongs to which pattern. A longstone or a broad-stone makes a fine gatepost now, remarkable in a country of wooden ones; but was the hedge aligned on it, or the stone brought from some-where else? In either case, what was it doing before? A circular treeless bank on the open moor may be a relic of fairly recent shepherding, or it may have been built three or four thousand years ago for a purpose we do not understand. A sunny slope showing traces of old walls may have been used and abandoned again and again in the forty or fifty centuries since the first farmers arrived.

So starting from chronology is not much help on the ground. The prehistoric 'ages' merged slowly not suddenly, and little scientific dating is available for Exmoor yet. It may be worth trying to see the monuments in relation to each other and to the hills and streams and the seasons, and taking seriously any link which seems to recur. Gradually a pattern may begin to appear.

Big Barrows

The characteristic Exmoor monuments are, of course, the great skyline barrows. Their profile is superb, almost unharmed, but nearly all have grassy pits in the middle, dug by tomb-robbers long ago. The shapes are known elsewhere—*bowl,* like a pudding-basin upside down, *bell,* a bowl with a narrow ledge round the base, and *disc,* the generic name for various circular platforms, standing very little above ground level, with a surrounding ditch or bank or both, and often a small mound some-where within the ring. Comparison with the magnificent Wiltshire barrows on Normanton Down or at the Winterbourne Stoke cross-roads near Stonehenge dates these to the peak of Bronze Age civilisation in southern England, about 1500 BC.

The best line of them curves for more than two miles along the south-west ridge of the moor, from Setta Barrow, through the high cluster of Five Barrows, to Two Barrows, and on to the small One Barrow at the eastern end of the ridge, about a quarter of a mile north of the county boundary road. There are more than twenty altogether, including bowl, bell, and several kinds of disc. Setta Barrow was for many cen-turies a boundary landmark of the Royal Forest, and when John Knight, a midland ironmaster, bought the Forest and built a wall round it, he

Five Barrows.

could not encroach on the common on the Devon side, and would not give up a few square yards of his Somerset estate to leave a great prehistoric tomb intact, but insisted—it is said—on driving his wall right through it. The deep cut is a sad testimony to greed.

No two barrows in this long line are exactly alike. Setta has the remains of a supporting ring wall, with horizontal walling and upright boulders slanting outward, pressed out by the weight of the great earthen mound. About a hundred paces to the SE another, a disc of some kind, has a hummock filling the NE quadrant; to anybody approaching uphill from the SW this—if it is original—would have been right of centre, breaking the nearby skyline; in fact a short row of stones leads up to it from the SW. These, and other stones encircling the disc, were plotted by Hansford Worth in 1905, and most of them were located again by probing in the winter of 1979-80, when they seemed, from the thickness of the turf, to have been buried for a long time. Further SE, near the road, another disc is ringed by a ditch, a low grass-covered wall, and some boulders. The Five Barrows (nine of them) are different again, bowls, bell and discs, and they include an interesting high flat ring with ditch and bank, particularly impressive when seen across the Kinsford valley on the way from Simonsbath. (Shapeless pits near it may indicate old mining tests.) Two of the bowl barrows, one at the

16

NW end of this group and a neat little one to the east, a princeling among potentates, seem to have been faced, or perhaps sprinkled, with small quartz stones. At the ancient Kinsford crossroads a sizeable circular platform was ploughed for the first time in 1977, and improvised excavation showed it to consist of a complete ring wall, 2 ft. high, enclosing a space some 21 paces across with a small cairn off-centre. This, too, was right of centre if seen against the skyline of the ridge from downhill, as would seem reverent, but the wall was uninterrupted. The cairn was shaped like the lower half of a beehive, and when complete would have stood about 5 ft. high. In the middle of it was a deep hole, empty except for the peaty topsoil, but of a shape and size to have held a cremation urn.

The next barrow south-eastward, close to the ridge road, may be another of the same kind; it looks much as Kinsford Barrow looked before ploughing, and on Dartmoor these 'ring-cairns', only recently being noticed on Exmoor, tend to occur in pairs. At Two Barrows (a group of at least four) a bowl barrow was cut to a half-circle when wall and road were made. Unfortunately this is not the only such occurrence; on the Exford-Withypool parish boundary, along the ridge north of Braddymoor, one of two bowl barrows now has only its southern half; the Exford side has been ploughed flat—perhaps an irrevocable loss in knowledge for an infinitesimal gain in food. The variety in the long line

Setta Barrow, with the boundary wall driven through it.

17

stretching both ways from Five Barrows shows the importance of keeping the whole series intact until proper investigation can be made. Any one of the tumuli may hold an important clue to the beliefs, changes in custom or distinctions of sex or social standing which determined the differences of form.

This line runs along the south-west rampart of the moor, looking across to Dartmoor, away SW to the Cornish hills, and out over Barnstaple Bay to Hartland Point and Lundy. Another fine series stretches east from Chapman Barrows along the central ridge, then seems to cease, but is resumed towards Dunkery, which looks both to Wales and the Quantocks. The Wambarrows on Winsford Hill border another ridgeway before it drops down to Dulverton, and they look north to Dunkery, west across all southern Exmoor, and south-west to Dartmoor. A more straggly line runs along the ridge of Molland Common, and yet another beside the coast road above Culbone. Unmistakably, these skyline positions were carefully chosen for important tombs.

Grave goods imply confidence in an after-life, but we do not know what was believed about the spirits of the dead. Did they go away on a long journey, or linger on the hill tops to watch over their people? Were they, like King Arthur, expected to come back to the rescue in time of great danger? There is no knowing. It is easier to guess the value of the high barrows to the living: landmarks visible for many miles, lookout points in peace or war, beacon sites for signalling news, as word of Agamemnon's victory at Troy was flashed homeward across sea and mountains to Mycenae. Who were these people's heroes? What tales did they tell or sing, by the fire on winter evenings? There seems not the faintest chance of that ever being known again.

Lesser Barrows

If there are fifty or sixty big skyline barrows, there are far more of medium size, about eight paces across, cleverly placed on false crests on the hillsides. Most of these are bowl barrows, and many are in poor condition. Sometimes a robber-pit, enlarged by rain and scuffed by animals, has caused collapse. If the barrow is near a road or a wall, stones may have been taken for re-use. Out on the open moor, some are debatable. Eighty years ago antiquarians tended to call them hut circles, even if there was no possible doorway. Later, some were explained as eroded bowl barrows—the classic of this re-interpretation is the 'hut circle' on the saddle of Cheriton Ridge. Still more recently, it is becoming clear that a few were not bowls but ring barrows or ring cairns, of Kinsford type but smaller. Some of these have an entrance through the circular wall—presumably for funeral rites—and some have not. An untypical one on the west slope of Ilkerton Ridge is more like the Scottish ring cairns; its uninterrupted wall is about 2 ft. high and three paces thick, apparently sloping inward, round a floor three paces across. Another, more like Kinsford but with an entrance, is on the county and Forest boundary at the southern end of Furzehill Common. It has a low thin ring wall, neatly built. Within the circle a small cairn, *left* of centre if one goes uphill to it through the south-eastern entry, is untidy now, but when it was domed or conical would, from that approach, have appeared against the skyline on a false crest. The Forest and county boundary here is marked only by 'lesser meare-stones', slabs about 2 ft. high pointing along the boundary line, and one of these stands in the prehistoric cairn, presumably placed there in Forest times to give it a little extra height, and help the men on ponies riding the bounds.

Sometimes, on the fringes of the moor, the middle-sized barrows have been regarded as expendable, and ploughed several times. Charles Whybrow excavated one such on Bratton Down in 1971, and described it in the 1977 edition of *Antiquary's Exmoor*. Its ditch enclosed a circular space almost 10 m. across, within which a cairn 6 or 7 m. in diameter had covered a burial, but most of the cairn stones had been removed and the whole wide mound was only a few inches high. The traces were of cremation—burnt earth and charcoal, a burial-pit dug when the funeral pyre had cooled, a smooth-topped stone forming the floor of the pit, and on the stone, fragments of burnt bone and of a broken pottery urn. A large stone which might have covered the pit lay nearby, but repeated ploughing had disturbed the whole site. Radio carbon analysis has since dated this barrow to the eleventh century BC.

Other Burials

Bronze Age burial customs did not remain unchanged through the centuries. Earlier, the Neolithic people had used communal tombs, burying the dead outstretched, or shuffling their dried-up bones into the burial chamber, hugger-mugger, sweeping older skeletons aside. The next comers introduced single burial, with the body crouched, knees to chin, lying on its side in a short rectangular stone coffin made of upright slabs with another as lid. (19th century antiquarians gave these coffins the Celtic name *kyst,* equivalent to English *chest,* though they are pre-Celtic by a great many centuries.) Usually a joint of meat was placed beside the corpse, and a beaker with drink for the journey; sometimes, too, a simple weapon of copper or flint. The drinking cups are the origin of the archaeological name 'Beaker Folk' for these people. A 'beaker' coffin was found very near to the coastal ridge road, at the head of Deddycombe, formerly part of Culbone parish, and is now on display in Taunton museum. Another, longer and empty, can be seen, though not very easily, in Langridge Wood near Treborough (the ridge motif again). It was found in 1820 by roadmen collecting surface stone, and the skeleton was respectfully reburied in Treborough church-yard.

Later, cremation replaced burial. Sometimes an urn stood upright, sealed, to preserve the burnt bones, and sometimes it was inverted over them. There was usually, though not always, a mound above this—an earthen one probably more often than a cairn, on Exmoor. The middle-sized barrows may have been for single burials, but some of the big ones are likely to have had other urns, perhaps those of relations or favourite followers, inserted later in their sloping sides. This is known elsewhere, and expresses of course a deep-seated human impulse. There was a variant in the *Iliad*. Achilles conducted princely funeral rites with a huge pyre, for his loved squire Patroclus, but arranged that the golden urn containing the burnt remains should have only temporary burial in a medium-sized barrow. His own death in front of Troy had been fore-told, and his friend's bones and his own were eventually to be mingled in that urn and placed in the splendid barrow he could confidently expect the Greeks to build for him.

Sometimes, in this country, the urn stood in a small pit below ground level, not always marked by a conspicuous barrow. There was only a low mound on the north-west slope of Bampfylde Hill, North Molton, where, during ploughing in 1889, the farmer's old white horse, Darling, put his foot into a hole and the ground gave way under him. The con-tents of the hole did not seem worth keeping, except for a necklace, given to Exeter Museum long afterwards. Its single amber bead must have been the wearer's treasure; some of the others were faience, some shale, or perhaps lignite, of local origin. Faience beads, formerly thought to denote trade with Egypt, now seem as likely to have been made in Britain. Even so, the necklace implies a little modest prosperity. Perhaps the presence of copper a mile or two away, in the Mole valley, had something to do with this.

A grave with no mound surviving was found in 1978, when Cyril Cole, of Lower Ash Moor Farm, Rose Ash, was reploughing old pasture on the north slope of the Chulmleigh-Dulverton ridge. The ploughshare dislodged a big stone; he stopped to investigate and found that it had covered the top of an upright pottery jar. He reported this at once, and generously postponed further work. Twelve days later a quick profes-sional excavation and study of the site was made by the Department of the Environment's Central Excavation Unit. The urn, now in Exeter museum, contained cremated bones, while oak charcoal had been used to fill the pit round it. Radio carbon dates it to the thirteenth century BC—about the middle of the Bronze Age. Big barrows along the ridgeway include two about half a mile east of the farmhouse on high ground, and another downhill, a little to the west, at Catkill Cross, but nothing else was found in the field.

Mounds

Some burials have no mounds, and there are also mounds which seem to be man-made, usually occur in groups near barrows, but may or may not contain burials. Nearly all these are about two paces across, and low, either flat or conical. Most are circular, but a few are oval, as though they were double graves. They tend to be drier than the land round them, and free of rush. They have not been convincingly explained as natural, nor as relics of any kind of farming. They began to be noticed as groups in 1975, during fieldwork on White Ladder near Five Barrows, but here and there one or two had been observed in apparent isolation, and taken to be small barrows. One such was excavated and recorded in 1905 by Chanter and Hansford Worth, but they destroyed it in the process. It was among the Chapman Barrows, close to a group of five standing stones, and revealed 'a small interment pit, without a cover, but containing charcoal'.

One of the large number near White Ladder was professionally excavated in autumn 1979, by John Rowley, from Hull, and it proved to be an earthen mound over a circular floor very loosely composed of small lumps of quartz, which lay on undisturbed soil. Nothing dated it. Even the question whether the stones were placed there by man or nature remained open. Other mounds nearby had seemed in fieldwork to be linked by two intersecting rows of quartz stones, regularly placed but mainly hidden under grassy turf, and some of the mounds were thought to have an outer ring, like a widely spaced necklace of white beads, at a standard distance from the centre. All this awaits investigation.

Meanwhile, similar groups had been noticed on Dartmoor, where nearly everything is made of stone, and they were recorded by Andrew Fleming, in the *Proceedings of the Devon Archaeological Society, 1980,* as cairnfields, like others known in the north of England. They tend to be near larger cairns, the equivalent of medium-sized barrows here. On Exmoor, moundfields seems a more accurate name; at least three have been identified so far, besides two single mounds among the Chapman Barrows—the one near the five stones, and another, very neat and shapely, close to the long line of big barrows.

The most interesting evidence here, at present, is the Neolithic to Bronze Age context in which the moundfields occur. One, on Ilkerton Ridge, may be simply a large cemetery. Along the ridge and its flanks are large and smaller barrows of several kinds, with a moundfield among them, and near the middle of it all, well placed to be seen from a

The Longstone, Challacombe, in winter.

distance, stands an elegant little longstone, as though marking the site. At the southern end, on the east slope, a space nearly surrounded by low remnants of wall strongly suggests Bronze Age cultivation. Although the mounds are scattered along the ridge and near the enclosure, there are none inside it. They consist of earth, not stone, so they are not clearance cairns, and they form no recognisable pattern.

Elsewhere, in three places, mounds, barrows, longstones and small stone settings together seem to be related to the lie of the land. These three—and there may well be others—are at Chapman Barrows, Five Barrows, and on the Portford side of Withypool Hill. It looks as if each of these was not only a cemetery, a 'God's acre' of its time, but also an important centre of worship. Who the gods were can only be guessed, but there is evidence for the sun, and for the sources of streams.

Sacred Areas

The best-known of these holy places—if that is what they were—is on the spine of the moor, above Challacombe. The impressive line of Chapman Barrows, visible for many miles, culminates to eastward in a large one excavated and recorded by Chanter in 1905, which contained 'a covered interment pit with charcoal and bone-ash'. Another, opened in 1885, had yielded 'an inverted urn and burnt bone'. Near this is the quincunx, the five-stone setting shown on the OS maps. It is a curious little group of small upright slabs, the four corners exactly north, south, east and west of the larger central stone where the diagonals would cross. The small mound excavated in 1905 lay 43 ft. NE of the eastern stone.

Further eastward along the ridge is an embanked space like a long blunt wedge, rounded at the corners, about 27 paces long and 10 across. Its origin and purpose are unknown, but the shape hints at Neolithic. Next is the tallest longstone on the moor, often called *the* Longstone; it stands near the saddle, in a shallow bog at the source of the river Bray, and points exactly down the stream. Beyond that the big Longstone Barrow, on a crest, and a few others, smaller and flatter, lead on to Woodbarrow, a fine conclusion. The Longstone is not on the ridge but on the spring-line.

On the southern flank are two settings of small stones. One is a row of three, alongside a contour track. They might be waymarks set up much later—but wouldn't *one* stone be enough for that? The second is a rectangle; of a probable four stones on either side only two are still erect, but others lie prone; the line of the formation runs up and down the slope. A third group stands not far from Woodbarrow on the Winaway side; it is nondescript now but may be the remnant of a more comprehensible pattern.

23

Heather and bog may hide much more, but the dozen or so big barrows along the ridge, the quincunx and at least two other stone settings, the two small mounds and the wedge-shaped enclosure, all within a mile or so of the Longstone, suggest that the ridge was very important. Was its sanctity derived from the springs of the Bray?

The line passing through Five Barrows holds a concentration of monuments at least as rich. Except for the big skyline barrows there is very little to see, but the hardly perceptible mounds and stones may be full of significance.

Again the middle part seems to be concerned with stones and water, but this time with midwinter sunrise as well. On the wide northern slope down from Five Barrows is an assembly of perhaps as many as fifty or sixty mounds, spread over firm ground between two boggy stream-heads. Across this, from one spring towards—but not quite as far as—the other, runs White Ladder, a double row of small standing stones, originally a quarter of a mile long. This was noticed, entirely by chance, after a cold late spring in 1975, when the grass was very short. Several quartz stones and some slabs of sandstone, protruding a few inches through the turf, formed a pattern regular enough to indicate that the spacing had been one stride across, and two between pairs. Further search and probing confirmed this ladder-like design, locating 71 visible stones, and a further 90 which were either submerged though still upright, or fallen and overgrown. (A few more were found later.) The uprights pointed *along* the line, and the slow process of probing and checking showed that there were no additional stones between the two rows nor immediately outside them. In other words, it had not been a wall or bank. Nor is it likely to have been set up as a boundary, since a single row with its stones much further apart would have been enough for that. Of the 161 stones found, 61 were quartz. The shining white stone was often used in prehistoric burial places, sometimes taken long distances for the purpose. It is a natural ingredient of this ridge, and that may have been one reason for the choice of site.

Known in Forest times as a landmark, named in the final perambulation record and shown on the 1819 Inclosure Map when the Crown land was sold, White Ladder was then forgotten except as a name. (Hunting people still sometimes speak of 'Whiteladders Combe' at the foot of the hill.) Grass grew over most of the stones, and in consequence a stretch near the middle was ploughed out unrecognised in 1970 or so; the farmer found the quartz boulders troublesome to extract. Another short piece, adjoining this, had been lost in road metalling about fifteen years earlier. There were probably once 200 pairs, and originally each stone would have stood about one foot high and one along.

24

Such avenues are common on Dartmoor, where big stones are plentiful, but few are as long as this, and most are at a lower altitude. On Dartmoor the row, single or double, often runs down from a small cairn to the side of a stream. White Ladder is almost level, but the incline is *up* from a low mound to a boggy source of Kinsford Water*—the highest obvious source, since the only higher one is deceptively swallowed for about half a mile. The stream runs from south to north—the direction which by Exmoor tradition gives it notable healing powers. A single stone lying under the peat bog at the head of the row is twice as big as the others, and different in shape.

The avenue stops at the stream-head, and points across it to where the sun would have risen on midwinter morning in about 2000 BC. To a primitive people the annual return of the sun, which had seemed to be leaving them as the days grew shorter and shorter, must have been supremely important. Some of the stone circles, including Stonehenge, show concern with the midwinter sunset—perhaps the really crucial time for supplication. Was there at White Ladder some solemn ceremony, at the source of the stream and the moment of midwinter sunrise, to implore the favour of the two great life-givers?

So far as is yet known, no other Exmoor monument reflects this anxiety. Conventionally, for lack of sure dating, these simple rows of small stones are considered to be very early Bronze Age or late Neolithic. The solstice sunrise date tallies with this, putting the whole thing to the beginning of the second millennium BC. If so, it would be five or six centuries older than the big skyline barrows. Sun and water might have been the first sanctifiers of the whole wide space.

A third area which may have been especially holy lies to the south and south-west of Withypool. Near Portford bridge is a large mound-field, including a cluster of three probable ring barrows, medium-sized, each appearing to have the remains of an off-centre cairn. It spreads across the saddle of a low ridge running from Green Barrow towards Withypool stone circle and the bowl barrow at the top of Withypool Hill. The dip of the saddle is alongside the headwaters of the Portford stream, and on a plateau on the opposite bank once stood a good slab of stone about three feet high. (Fred Milton, a Withypool farmer,

KINSFORD, earlier Kensford and Kentsford, implies a river name like the Kennett in Suffolk, crossed by the Icknield Way beside some barrows at Kentford, and the Avebury Kennet, which in Roman times was pronounced *Cunet(io)*. It must be one of the very oldest river names; in Sanskrit *Kunti* was a spring, and still, in Hindi, Kunti is a girl's name and the village well is a *Kund*. The stream rising at White Ladder is Kinsford Water, though before joining the Barle ('Beorg-wella', Saxon for 'hill spring') it becomes Sherdon Water, formerly Shirburn (Saxon 'sheer', or 'pure', stream). Perhaps respect for the spring lasted a long time, and preserved the pre-Saxon name up by the stones.

The Harepath in Birch Cleeve, Simonsbath.

remembers the stone well; he says it was removed during road alterations in the 1920s.)

Until this group was recognised it had seemed strange that there was not more to be seen in the neighbourhood of the stone circle. It is still odd that so little has been reported near Dunkery, the highest hill top on the moor, and the most frequented.

Henges and Stone Circles

Earthen mounds, cairns, rings of earth and stone; upright stones, single or in patterns; any of these may hint at the beliefs and religious customs of Neolithic or Bronze Age people. But some of them may have been set up much later, for quite different reasons; and there may have been other monuments made of timber, as were Woodhenge in Wiltshire and Arminghall in Norfolk, and now completely lost. (An excavating archaeologist has to watch for the slightest traces of wood, or stains left by copper or iron weapons or ornaments eaten away by the acid peat. One of the objections to 'treasure-hunting' with metal-detectors is that clues of that kind are lost.)

The distinction between henges and stone circles is not clearcut. The name *henge* started as the early English name for Stonehenge, describing the stone lintels 'hung' across the uprights. But since both there and at Avebury the ring of stones is enclosed by ditch and bank, archaeologists now call this kind of circle a *henge,* whether it contains a stone ring or not, and reserve the name *stone circle* for those without earthworks. The simple earthen henges are commonest in the lowlands, where there is little stone, while on granite moors with little topsoil a token 'wall' of spaced uprights is more frequent. The Wiltshire Downs have the splendid architecture of Avebury and Stonehenge, and also the grassy henges of Marden a few miles from Avebury and Durrington in the neighbourhood of Stonehenge. These embankments now enclose huge empty circles, but once contained rings of wooden posts; they seem to belong to a remoter epoch, still harder to understand. On Dartmoor and Bodmin Moor the stone circles are made of granite pillars and slabs, taller than a tall man and visible from a long way away. On Exmoor there is nothing so impressive. Stone for big monoliths is scarce, and there may not have been the manpower, or the organisation, or perhaps even the motive, for carrying it very far. All we have is a probable earthen henge, and two unmistakeable circles of small sandstone slabs.

The probable henge is in two fields at Woolhanger, Parracombe, not far from a flint-knapping floor at Ranscombe head. A circle of flat ground was once surrounded by a ditch, and outside that by an earthen bank. A hedge now divides the site, and though the north-eastern half is still handsome, the south-western has been ploughed out. Fortunately air photographs show traces which complete the ring, and it is important not to lose these. At present this is the only recognised Neolithic monument on Exmoor, and it may be a valuable clue. It is about a mile north of Chapman Barrows and the western end of the ridge. It may mean that the area was thought sacred even before the Bronze Age people arrived.

The larger of the two stone circles, about the same size as the Woolhanger henge, is on the south-west slope of Withypool Hill. The other, smaller but built of rather bigger stones, is close to the road bridge over Colley Water on Porlock Common, south of the old flint-knapping site at Hawkcombe Head. Both have some stones fallen, and some missing, but are quite clearly rings. A third setting of comparable size on Almsworthy Common, near the head of Chetsford Water, is more problematic. From uphill, NW, it looks circular, but from nearby it is not so simple. The stones point in various directions, and some are inside the apparent circumference. It has been seen as concentric ellipses and even as a series of parallel rows. Perhaps too few stones survive for interpretation ever to be convincing. Some may lie under the thin turf, some may have been taken to build the old field boundaries—perhaps prehistoric—which have recently been found close by.

There are rumours recorded of lost circles on Mattocks Down in the north-west, and near Dun's Stone south of the Brendons ridgeway in the east, but little is left at either except a large standing stone. One would expect more circles, among so many barrows, but at present (1982) only the Withypool and Porlock ones are certain.

Neither of these has been excavated. Each is near a barrow—a small one just outside the Porlock ring and a big one on Withypool Hill. The Porlock stones stand on a little ledge above the bank of Colley Water, near its source; Withypool Circle is further up a slope near the head of Westwater. Both have access to either one or two ancient thoroughfares. Hawkcombe Head is near the coastal ridge and might also have been approached from the south, past Lucott Cross and over Colley Water. Withypool Circle could be reached from the south-west ridgeway via Green Barrow, or from the Wambarrows highway just across the Barle.

Association with stream-heads and ridge roads may or may not bear on the really interesting questions—what the stone circles were, who used them, how and why. These riddles are not yet fully answered anywhere, though more and more has been ascertained by skilful and patient investigation during the last few decades. Two books by Aubrey Burl, *Rings of Stone* and *The Stone Circles of the British Isles,* describe some of the results. The henges and circles—almost peculiar to Britain—are now seen to vary in age, design, and usage. Some, including Stonehenge, were altered more than once to suit changing religious customs, and perhaps secular purposes too, in the two thousand years or so of their validity. There is certainly no single explanation to suit them all.

So one has to cast about in search of light. The henges must have been reserving a space for something. In Cumbria they are near to known prehistoric highways used for the Neolithic axe trade. The strong stone which made the best axes was taken very long distances, and the importance of a good axe is easy to understand. It cut and shaped timber for building, it cleared woodland for ploughing, it would brain an ox for food and leather, or chop off an enemy's head. Local people from a long way round would gather at agreed points on the route, at agreed times of the year, to barter the axes, and as at an autumn sheep fair still, the gathering would become a social event. It would be strange if the big religious ceremonies, whatever they may have been, were not held at the same time and place; the choice of time may have been like the twofold observance of Lady Day or Michaelmas, very much later.

If mortals used the ring for dealings with their gods (as indicated in some circles, but not all, by the remains of gifts and sacrifices) the barriers of earth and water may have been to keep good spirits in and bad spirits out. Later a ring of stones was added, or used alone, since even the dullest of immortals would know that spaced stones facing inward meant a wall. The sanctity or magic might accumulate in various ways. Some stone circles are clearly related to the sun, especially at its midsummer and midwinter halts, and some to the moon. Given the widespread country belief that any plant or animal grows best under the waxing moon, and given the coastwise fisherman's dependence on the tides, it may have been nearly as important to secure the moon's favour as the sun's. Besides, the moon is strong when men are asleep and helpless. Very potent objects were buried in some of the circles— notably the strong axes, which remained valuable long after Neolithic times. There was even a *token* axe, made of chalk, buried edge-upwards at Stonehenge, as well as axe heads pecked out on some of the sarsens. Sometimes there are human burials in small cairns inside the circle, and sometimes traces of fire, with animal bones, implying sacrifice rather than a funeral pyre. There is also evidence now and then of human sacrifice—headless corpses—and, particularly horrible, the sacrifice of children and infants. Perhaps an angry or jealous god could only be appeased by what was very hard to give, the loved son or daughter, Isaac or Iphigenia; and the bones show that at Woodhenge there was no angel or ram, no goddess in a cloud, to save the child from slaughter.

Culbone Row.

The signs point to a grim belief that life must be bought by death, as Persephone, daughter of the corn goddess, was snatched to the underworld for half the year but rose again in spring. It seems, too, that some kind of Eleusinian mysteries may have been performed in the circle—perhaps erotic dances to induce fertility. Here and there a stone circle had a central stone, with a few bones buried at its foot. Perhaps some ceremony enacted there was the remote origin of dancing round the maypole. Many stone circles have names or legends referring to men or girls turned into stone for dancing on a Sunday—tales spread, perhaps, by the Christian clergy to warn people off old practices which seemed evil? At Avebury some form of pagan worship was going on as late as the 14th century AD, in spite of the church built at the edge of the circle to neutralise its power. Then the clergy arranged for the great sarsen stones to be loosened and buried. When one of them fell too quickly and crushed an educated helper to death, the demolition ceased. One can almost hear what the sullen onlookers muttered.

None of this tells us what took place in Withypool and Porlock circles, but small though these are, they belonged to the same tradition. At any time some further find of small stone emplacements or low earthworks, or a hitherto unnoticed relationship, may set them in the larger context and explain their use.

Stone Rows

Some of the great stone circles have long broad avenues linking them with water. At Callanish a straight avenue leads down to the sea, at Avebury a zigzag one goes downhill to the river Kennet. On Dartmoor smaller stones, paired in narrow avenues or singly spaced in long rows, often lead from streams up to small barrows; alternatively, one end may be blocked by a tall stone set athwart the line. Were the dead being given access to running water, along a path defined by the stones? Did stones and water confine a wandering spirit? Conjecture can be fascinating, but the hope of really knowing what it all meant is slender. If only these people of three or four thousand years ago had left some record in words!

So far, very few long rows have been recognised on Exmoor, and the first one reported is increasingly a matter of doubt. This is Corney's Row on Wilmersham Common, noticed after swaling in 1966. It runs uphill for about 60 metres very irregularly, single and double, then swerves some 30° and spreads out into three or four twisting lines. The small stones point across as well as along the row, and three taller ones mark the ends and the turning-point. It has no obvious connection with water or with any barrow or mound. At first it seemed to be an authentic stone row, a rather poor relation of the many on Dartmoor. But on later visits Corney also noticed, not far away on Honeycombe Hill, the remains of old banks of stone and earth forming a rectangle and a ring, and a revetted straight bank of much the same length as the row which he had recorded in the *Exmoor Review* of 1967. These later finds suggested farming and a homestead, and he reported them in another article in the *Review* in 1968. Recent air photographs, confirming them, strengthen the alternative hypothesis, that the 'row' is a dilapidated field wall of the same period.

A row which Charles Whybrow recorded in 1970 as near the 6-stone Pinford setting and similar to Corney's has lately eluded persistent search, both before and after swaling; and it is known that nothing has been removed. He described a double row, 54 ft. long and about 2 ft. wide, with 19 stones visible. In conversation he showed its position, on a 2½ ins map, as south of the setting and in the angle between two streams. Prehistoric field boundaries were not much regarded on Exmoor until recently, but in the last few years practised field workers have noticed several ruined stony banks, very low now, on the hill between the two Pinfords. It is possible that this 'row' was a 54 ft. length of boundary, which such a careful observer as Charles would have interpreted differently now. He would have been quick to say that it cannot really count as a stone row until it has been identified again.

White Ladder near Five Barrows, rediscovered in 1975, has already been described. Its length and regularity are good, and its relationship with sun and water seems important, though the paired stones are inconspicuous almost to vanishing point. The most recently found, a single row on Culbone Hill, almost hidden in dense woodland, is far more dramatic.

No rider could penetrate the tangle of dwarfed and twisted pines, and few walkers would, which must be why the row has escaped notice for so long. Then lately three people, independently and in quick succession, stumbled upon it by chance. One was the Ordnance Survey archaeologist, Norman Quinnell, whose plan and record were printed in the *Proceedings of the Somerset Archaeological Society 1981* (published in 1982) and the second, a visitor from Bristol, J. E. Hancock, who reported it orally. The third was Ernest Mold of Lynton, who described the find in an article in the *Exmoor Review* 1983 (also published in 1982). The spacing of the stones, too close for boundary markers, and their alignment, too consistent for a wall, leave no doubt that this is a prehistoric single row, like the ones familiar on Dartmoor.

At least twenty grey-brown stones are still visible. Most of them stand about knee-high. Two very small ones close together look like triggers, unwisely placed on the uphill side of their sandstone slab which, lacking proper support, now lies flat under dark loose soil. The space between the identified uprights varies between two and fifty-four strides, in a west-east line about 400 yards long—much the same length as White Ladder. It runs along the contour through the tangled wood, then, east of a lane, climbs slightly across open ground where the surviving stones are fewer and bigger.

To the west, through the trees, the row points directly to a good bowl barrow, in a clearing some 150 yards away. It is not in sight, but the line was checked very carefully on the difficult ground by two experienced field workers in January 1982. Eastward, the last stone is near a newer plantation on the crest of a hill; a less shapely barrow, of similar size, about 250 yards further on, is on the far slope and not visible from the row. It may belong to a different group, further downhill. Each stone points east-west, unmistakably though not precisely. In the wood it is hard to know whether the whole line is as straight as it seems, but the survey plan shows it wavering in a shallow arc whose ends curve up just to the north of east and north of west. Perhaps simple people were building it in early summer, aiming at the sunrise and sunset positions which they could see every day but which changed imperceptibly as their work went on? If that was so, they must have begun in the middle, and set up the row first, then the barrow.

At the western end the line runs near a probably prehistoric ridgeway—as does White Ladder. When the ridge divides, the road swerves south-east on the highest ground while the row keeps on to the east. There is no stream, but might not the stone row leading up from a western barrow towards sunrise over a hill mean that the sun was to renew life in the dead? Christians still bury a body with its feet to the east, ready for resurrection.

The new discovery of the prehistoric row raises fresh questions about the Culbone Stone, known since 1940, when it was found lying face downward and re-erected, as an inscribed stone of the Dark Ages. It stands some 70 paces SW of what seems now to be the western end of the row, and appears unrelated to it. It points NE and SW, parallel with the parish boundary which has been following the row westward but has now turned south-west to run inland, along a low bank. It is very much like the stones of the row except for one important thing—the carving on its SE face.

That is a wheeled cross, stylistically dated to the sixth or seventh century when it was not uncommon to incise the symbol on standing stones. There are several on Lundy, more in Cornwall, and a great many in Wales. The unusual feature of this one is that it is *askew* on its upright stone. Within the circle, which is about 3½ ins in diameter, the cross is neither upright nor diagonal, neither St. George's nor St. Andrew's; its top quadrant is like ten minutes to one, and the stem,

The Wheeled Cross Stone, Culbone.

equal in length to the diameter, projects from what would be the four on a clock. This is not clumsiness; the circle and straight lines are the work of a good craftsman. Then why? It seems, at best, disrespectful.

The stone must have been almost beside the coastal ridge road, which was marked in the Bronze Age by barrows, and recorded in mediaeval perambulations of the Forest. The likelihood is that the track—it would be no more—was also used during the intervening Dark Ages, when tradition says that a Welsh holy man, Beuno, founded Culbone church (Kil Beun). The stem of the cross points down to the NE, which is the way to the church. One possibility is that a stone was taken from the prehistoric row and set up near the road to guide travellers to the tiny Christian settlement. The line of the stone would be enough for local people who knew that the church was not inland but far down the steep slope to the sea; perhaps the slant of the stem was to help strangers.

Stone Settings

Quite different from either the long rows or the circles are the small stone settings, Exmoor's special puzzle. Nearly thirty are known, but none are understood. They consist of anything from two or three to a dozen brown or grey slabs of sandstone, knee-high or less. Some are rectangles formed by two, three or four parallel rows, but some are more perplexing. At least five of them have one stone very much bigger

34

than any of its company. Usually the two-row settings have three or four stones on either side, each slab pointing along the line, and the rows are well apart, making a squat shape like a double square; those at Tom's Hill and West Pinford (East is a misnomer) are the best known of this type, and both are shown on the OS maps. In some, six or eight stones are still upright, though hard to find when heather and bracken are high, but more often several have fallen and lie flat. Where an almost regular pattern seems to need another stone, it may be perceptible just under the turf; in drought a patch of starved grass will betray it, or in wet weather you may feel it through the soles of your boots.

It is important to allow for stones being overgrown, shaly ones decomposing, and good ones having been removed for use elsewhere. Two settings marked on the 6 ins maps, one at the top of Hoscombe and one above Dippers' Combe on Swap Hill, have lately become rather less incomprehensible by a little probing. One had appeared as an incomplete circle with an 'outlier', the other as two rows of three with a much bigger stone outside the middle pair. Both, in fact, seem to have been three rows of three, evenly spaced and well aligned. Plotting and periodic checking are useful, because the stones are vulnerable, especially to shepherding by Land Rover. The visible pattern changes, making the earlier record important. But a description in geometrical terms of what can be seen today is no evidence of prehistoric design. Very careful excavation of the area within the stone pattern and a little beyond it might provide hints of the original purpose; probably several would have to be examined before even a good hypothesis could be made, let alone a reliable explanation.

Bearing all these reservations in mind, we still try to guess the riddle from the surviving stones. There is hardly any help from analogy; hesitant comparison has been made with the Scottish monuments called 'four-posters', but the resemblance is slight. The Scottish ones are squares or rectangles four or five paces each way, with a bulky stone at each corner. A few have been excavated, and most of these had cremation urns buried at their centre—as though squares had become customary instead of circles, with the enclosed space still the important thing. This might explain the two-row rectangles on Exmoor, but those composed of three or four rows leave little space and no dominant position within the frame. Others are short single rows of three, and some of the larger non-rectangular patterns are completely enigmatic.

There is no consistent orientation, but the shapes often point along a ridge or flank, or straight up and down the slope. They tend to be above the combes, and so situated that people performing any ceremony there could be seen from an opposite hillside. Some are surprisingly close together. At least three lie along or near the crest of Cheriton Ridge.

The Foreland   The   Severn

1056´

E.Lyn

1431´

R.Heddon

a

W.Lyn

b

R.Bray

1599   The Chains

1572

R.Exe

15

R.Barle

Kinsford Water

1404´

c

R.Bray

Danes Brook

3

R.Mole

R.Yeo

R.Mole

Crooked Oak

1

R.Mole

2

R.Taw

36

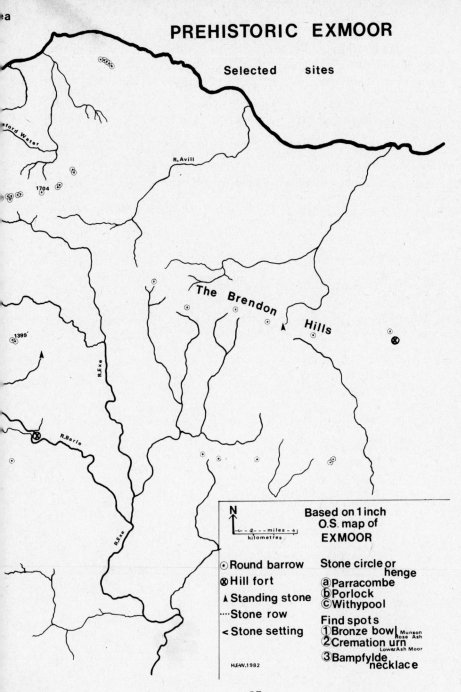

PREHISTORIC EXMOOR

Selected   sites

Based on 1 inch
O.S. map of
EXMOOR

N

←--2---miles--→
kilometres

⊙ Round barrow
⊗ Hill fort
▲ Standing stone
···· Stone row
< Stone setting

Stone circle or
         henge
ⓐ Parracombe
ⓑ Porlock
ⓒ Withypool

Find spots
① Bronze bowl Munson
                Rose Ash
② Cremation urn
                Lower Ash Moor
③ Bampfylde
        necklace

H.J.E-W.1982

A small stone setting, Brendon Common.

From Brendon Common to Swap Hill at least ten are dotted about, within sight of each other or not far away, and there are very probably more to be found. If they were all designed for the same purpose (but they may not have been) and if they were roughly contemporary (but perhaps they were centuries apart) the comparative nearness needs explanation. Were there so many people that each family had its own . . . its own what? Place of sacrifice? Of worship? Its household gods? Or were the settings used by a larger community to honour a whole range of divinities? Or had they magical properties? Three, and thrice three, persist in mythology, fairy tales and ballads. And there are Macbeth's witches, the three weird sisters, or fates, who, hand in hand, move round chanting,

> Thrice to thine, and thrice to mine,
> And thrice again, to make up nine.
> Peace! The charm's wound up.

Again, the quincunx near Chapman's Barrows—if that is the complete shape—may have expressed a belief which lingered on obscurely for a very long time. In the 17th century Sir Thomas Browne described an old charm against weeds; a chalked tile was placed at each corner of the field and one in the middle, and this, he said, 'though ridiculous in the intention, was rational in the contrivance, and a good way to diffuse the magick through all parts of the area'.

It is tantalising to have only hints and guesses about these strange little monuments. Some first-rate investigation is the next need.

Long Stones and Others

The single standing stones are a different kind of puzzle. A few are geological outcrops, like the Simonsbath 'White Rocks' in the wooded combe beside the church. Any stone of manageable size may have been moved from a forgotten prehistoric site and re-used for a purpose now superseded in its turn; whatever their first use was, the two fine slabs at Robber's Bridge show by their hinge and latch marks that the valley road was gated, not so very long ago. The big stone on Mattocks Down survives from a lost pattern, and so may others. But many must have been placed as markers of something or other, and the reason is sometimes known.

Some are Forest boundary stones; these may be large ones, mentioned by name in the records of Forest perambulations, or may be 'lesser meare-stones', added from time to time by the borderers. Some of the named stones are at three-parish corners; four of these, along the SW boundary, are particularly interesting. They are the Hooked Stone (Hawkridge, Withypool, Exmoor) and the Longstone at Sandyway,

West Pinford, a better preserved setting.

39

(Twitchen, North Molton, Exmoor) both now lost; the Horsehead Stone, perhaps identified in 1975, built into a wall where North Molton, High Bray and Exmoor meet; and the Longstone alias Hore Stone alias Lewcombe Stone, in Lewcombe north of Moles Chamber. Inscribed 'Fortescue' and miscalled Sloley Stone on the maps, this marks the corner of High Bray, Challacombe and Exmoor. It is a boulder rather than a longstone, and tucked down at the stream-head it would be difficult to see; but it may have been there for a different purpose in older times. The Sandyway and Horsehead Stones stood just below the watershed, near stream-heads, along a part of the prehistoric ridgeway which the makers of the mediaeval boundary followed. The lost Hooked Stone was well above the present spring-line at a curious kink in the boundary, as though two landmarks had identified the corner where perambulations often began and ended. It remains a puzzle. Foresters and commoners chose to use the barrows along the contour—Two Barrows, Kinsford and Setta, not Five Barrows or One Barrow which would involve a detour and an unnecessary climb. It would be troublesome to drag big stones up to an arbitrary boundary; more probably they were already standing there, and perhaps the streams show why.

The 'lesser meare stones' are easy to recognise, and are certainly mediaeval or later. They are small slabs or thin columns of brown or grey sandstone, usually about knee high. Sometimes they have one or two packing-stones at foot, and stand in a slight hollow, trodden by sheep who have gone round and round rubbing their backs against the stone—which must have been very firmly implanted. The OS maps show them separately and precisely as boundary stones, and they always point along the boundary line they define. The spacing is reasonable—not over-frequent, but enough to reassure. Good stretches of them run north from Edgerley Stone, east from Saddle Stone, and northward over difficult ground from Alderman's to Black Barrow.

In the West Kennet avenue at Avebury long stones are paired with broad, and alternated, and the same man-woman symbolism can be seen in some other circles and rows in the stony north and west. Broadstones are infrequent on Exmoor, though not unknown (here and there a big square slab can be seen beside a ridgepath, drilled for gate hinges). None survive in partnership with longstones, as far as is known, but a fine pair of them stands on Porlock Common. These are the Whitstones, massive sandstone slabs a foot thick, silvery grey in some lights and dull in others, slanting eastward, side by side, and unlike anything else on the moor.

Both would have stood at least five feet high when they were upright. One is a square-topped rectangle, 3 ft. wide, and the other, south of it, has a base rather more than 5 ft. wide but narrows gradually to a broad blunt triangle. Both are aligned a little east of north, with a space of 8 ft. between them, making in all a line some 16 ft. long. This does not appear to point to any natural landmark or known prehistoric site, but there is no evidence that the stones are outcrop. They stand some way down an eastward slope, high on the north side of Hawkcombe; from a little further down they are in broad silhouette against the skyline, and again from part of the coast road as it climbs east to Porlock Hill, but not from the crest of that road, and not from the combe. Eight paces down-hill, east and very slightly south of the southern stone, is a hummock which might be a small round barrow with a tomb-robber's pit in the centre of it.

One recent misconception has tended to darken counsel, and should be cleared out of the way. The broadstones stand on a spur where the old Porlock-Barnstaple bridlepath and the present Exford road leave the coastal highway, and they must always have been a welcome land-mark at that bleak corner, deserving a distinctive name. But they can never have been on the Forest boundary, nor were they the same as the 'Five Stones' of the mediaeval documents. Confusion about this has come from a reference in 1219 AD when, after Magna Carta, King John's vast encroachment to Selworthy and Wootton Courtenay was annulled, and a special perambulation was made in order to define the restricted boundary. The record names a 'Whiteston', *singular, not plural,* somewhere between County Gate and Hawkcombe Head. The natural contour line from the west swings south at Pittcombe Head, where a broad track still runs to the top of Hawkcombe. It is nearly a mile short of the Whitstones. In 1279 the same boundary line was defined as County Gate—Fifstane—Hawkcombe Head. (Fifstane is good vernacular for a plural when the number is given; until decimalisation one could weigh ten stone or use a three-foot rule, and it is still normal to live to three score years and ten.) A later perambulation, in 1300, marked a further contraction of the Forest, which no longer included Hawkcombe; it was ridden anti-clockwise, going from Alderman's Barrow via Black Barrow, and the record of it shows quite clearly that the Five Stones were west of Lillycombe Head. John Fortescue, in his *Stag-hunting on Exmoor,* 1887, says they were where the old Culbone/Oare boundary crossed the main road, 'where Deddycombe cot stood'. This places them near the stream-head and the Beaker grave found in 1896— in the quarry north of the roadside, according to local tradition—and suggests Bronze Age significance. At that site, they would have been a good landmark for the perambulations. But no boundary riders would have gone out eastward along the narrow tongue of undulating waste-land to the Whitstones and back in order to get from County Gate to Hawkcombe Head.

41

Why the stones were erected, and when, is still unknown. They are at the edge of a large area in which prehistoric people were active; flints were knapped only a mile away at Hawkcombe Head, and beyond that is the Porlock stone circle; they are close to the coastal ridgeway, with Culbone Row not two miles to the west, and big barrows beyond that leading to Deddycombe. There are possible affinities in Scotland and Wales; but the meaning has yet to be found.

Sometimes tall stones marked long tracks, much as milestones did on rough roads elsewhere; but again the question is 'when?' North of the Chains, a route from Hoar Oak herdings runs along the east side of Furzehill ridge past Roborough Castle and over Lyn Down towards the coast. Three times it passes gateposts which look like Bronze Age standing stones, about shoulder height. All three—two of them longstones and one broad—are drilled to take gate hinges; each is in a hedge-line and points along the track. The hedges must be 19th century, but the Day and Masters Somerset map of 1782 shows a road from Exe Head (*not* from Simonsbath, but branching off a lost road from Edgerley Stone to Black Pits) reaching the Forest and County boundary at Hoar Oak. This may or may not have run along Furzehill Common. If it did, the subsequent enclosure hedges may have been aligned on waymarking single stones, which were pressed into new service as gateposts. Further north, on Lyn Down, two longstones remaining from a row point in the same direction. Whenever a track from end to end of that long ridge was first thought necessary, markers would be needed too, in mist or rough weather—and good tall ones, not lesser meare-stones. Bronze Age barrows show well on a false crest, on a southward slope, at the Lynton end—they are miscalled hut circles on the map—and near them recent ploughing has left a great deal of surface stone. An odd-shaped setting of eight or ten stones stands on the eastern flank, and a number of single uprights are dotted about the ridge. Whether the gate stones were set up in their present position during the Bronze Age, or were moved there much later, perhaps in mediaeval or Tudor times, to guide shepherds leaving the Forest, we may never know. The latter seems more likely. Bronze Age people had sunshine and blue skies most of the time, and could rely on the northern barrows or the southern hill tops to show them their way.

A few single stones offer possible clues but not answers. The elegant little longstone on Ilkerton Ridge seems to mark a cemetery. Three in different fields close to North Molton face the noonday sun, their shoulders pointing exactly east and west. Two of them are nearly opposite each other across a dry valley; the third is on a hillside further north-west, and stands on a ledge below the crest, cutting the skyline if it is seen from downhill where two streams meet. Farmers agree that the precise alignment makes an origin as rubbing stones unlikely—and wooden rubbing posts are much more usual. Excavation of a single upright is seldom informative, for technical reasons; so one can only hope that if the stones are carefully preserved somebody, some day, will suddenly realise what they once meant.

Stones and Streams

A connection between standing stones and stream-heads seems to recur: White Ladder leading to the source of Kinsford Water; the Longstone at the head of the Bray; the stone which used to stand above Portford stream; Horsehead and Lewcombe, smaller but well sited, and perhaps the lost Sandyway Longstone. A sturdy one, hip high, stands at the source of the Heddon, pointing downstream. And there are others.

For Bronze Age men and women on Exmoor, as for everybody always and everywhere, water must have been close second to the sun as a life-giver—and either without the other could kill. Their climate was warmer and drier than ours; there was less peat; springs would rise clear and run quickly down the combes. To this day a deep unfailing spring is gratefully treasured in a year of drought. Longstone Wells, a farm near North Molton, has one of these. The well is in a corner of the farmyard; the stone is lost—very likely used in building long ago—but the name is old.

Greece had its river gods and nymphs from very early times. The Nile and the Ganges were holy rivers long before iron was used on their shores. In Britain nobody disputes that the Iron Age Celts worshipped streams. The best evidence near Exmoor is the Iron Age bowl of Glastonbury type which was found under the bog of a stream-head high on Crooked Moor,* Rose Ash; and it is interesting that as his mechanical digger worked to and fro clearing the peat, the Munson farmer, Bernard Ayre, noticed that it sliced off successive remnants of a long-rotted wooden post, upright, and three or four inches thick. Until the bowl appeared in the upcast the wood had no great significance, and he could not be sure of the relative positions; but the post certainly stood near the spring, and the bowl, which has a single ring-shaped handle, may once have been hung from it.

Belief in holy wells or springs is very much older than Christianity in this country, though how far back in prehistory it originated is not known. The Exmoor stones seem to offer at least a strong probability that Bronze Age people held some of their streams in great honour.

* CROOKED MOOR and CROOKED OAK, names sounding as playful as an English nursery rhyme, are really much older and very prosaic. *Cruc* was a hill in Celtic languages, and Oak may be a late rationalisation of the very common Saxon river-name *Yeo*, which meant simply 'Water'. The names Yeo Bridge and Yeo Barton at the foot of the hill make this seem likely.

Bronze bowl from Munson, Rose Ash.

Not all longstones are at stream-heads, and not all the innumerable springs have barrows or stone monuments particularly near them, but where the connection does occur it looks significant. Three especially— Buttery Stone, West Anstey Longstone, and the Caratacus stone on Winsford Hill—have resemblances with the Longstone at the source of the Bray.

The Buttery Stone is a slab protruding slightly from the boundary wall beside the ridge road at Buttery Corner, about a mile south-east of Two Barrows. (It is not mentioned in the perambulations, though Buttery Corner is; 'Buttewerthe' farm is very old, and was always just outside the Forest, bordering or *abutting* on it). The stone is at the head of a stream which once carved a deep combe straight down south-westward towards Heasley Mill, and, like the Challacombe Longstone, it points down the combe, not along the ridge. Far downhill, the stream is joined by another, from the east, wider but not appreciably longer, which is now mapped as the main stream of the Mole, and they run on SW together. The Mole was once called Nymet, a prehistoric name meaning holy, or divine, surviving in the Nympton village names further down its course.* If Bronze Age people, working straight upstream, thought this the real source of their holy river, the position of the Buttery Stone would be on their skyline, and it would invite the reverence of travellers passing along the ridgeway. Like so much else, this is only 'if'. But it might have been. Further downstream, a tributary of the Mole/Nymet has one source in a holy well near North Molton, and still further on the Munson stream flows into it as part of the water of Crooked Oak.

Very persuasive indeed is the shapely little longstone at the head of Longstone Combe on West Anstey Common. It is downhill from the ridge road, not far from the West Anstey skyline barrows. Approached from uphill or from either side it is well below the horizon and not remarkable. But is stands on a tiny bluff immediately above the spring,

* NYMET. In Sanskrit *Nimi* was a royal name. There was also a word *nimna,* low ground, which had compounds meaning river, lord of rivers, and son of *the* river (the Ganges). In later Indo-European languages *nim* words meant holy, or noble, or divine—like the Greek nymphs—and by Celtic times they were often linked also with water. Nimue the enchantress served the Lady of the Lake, Arnemetia presided over the healing springs at Buxton and must surely have been the Celtic water-goddess Anu, whom the Christian church disguised as St. Anne. A tribe called Nemetes lived beside the Rhine, and two *Nymet* rivers flowed into the Taw (a Yeo at Nymet Bridge, and the Mole at King's Nympton).

This link has been overshadowed by the related Gaullish word *nemeton,* a holy *place,* specifically a sacred grove or a shrine. The syllable *ton* or *dun* for a place was Indo-European too, and reappears in English names, as in the lands reserved for King, Queen and Bishop in the fertile valley of the Nymet/Mole below Bishop's Nympton. These names have misled enquirers. A fourth Nympton is more accurately called Nymet St. George, and this, like Nimete, the old name of Warkleigh on the right bank, helps to distinguish holy river from sacred grove. The Yeo/Nymet has Nymet or Nymph names dotted along its course, and no *Nymptons* at all.

45

Longstone, West Anstey; from the combe.

Longstone, West Anstey; from uphill.

pointing down the combe, which runs straight for a considerable distance, and from downstream it is against the skyline. In summer a hawthorn half conceals it, but in winter its whole height is silhouetted against the southern sky. The stream is only a small tributary of the Danesbrook, but like Kinsford Water at the head of White Ladder, and like the streamlet on Crooked Moor where the Munson bowl was found, it runs in the traditionally potent direction, from south to north.

A longstone much like it in height and shape and colour stands near Spire Cross on Winsford Hill. (*Cross,* as usual on Exmoor, means only a cross-roads; it is a description to help travellers, and is often named from a farm to which the side road leads. *Spire* refers to spiky rushes, as does the *Lis* of Liscombe; peat must have been muffling the stream by Saxon times). The stone, aslant now, stands just below the saddle but above the modern ridge road, not far from the Wambarrows. It points down a dry gutter or sunk path, of unknown origin, to a rushy bog from which a stream now flows past Higher and Lower Spire and Liscombe farms to join the Barle at Tarr Steps. All this might suggest a Bronze Age stream-head stone.

Two later events have engendered other ideas. Standing close to the mediaeval 'great way', the stone was named as a Forest boundary mark, the Langeston, in 1219. (Although King John's encroachments had been annulled, his father's and his brother's still held, so Withypool and Hawkridge remained in the Forest until 1301). The stone was already old. It bears a Latin inscription, datable to the Dark Ages, which is read as 'Carataci nepus'; perhaps 'clansman of Caratacus' would translate it best. So it is commonly called the Caratacus Stone, and assumed to have been erected beside the ridgeway either by or in compliment to Caradoc's relation, somewhere about 500 AD. But while the inscription is certainly of that time, the stone may have stood there much longer. It might have been set for the water-spirit some two thousand years before the Celtic leader's tribesmen passed that way.

In modern thinking, a column or statue is a tribute, but was it always as detached as that? If this was indeed stream worship, perhaps the second millennium people put up the stone to represent the god or goddess, who was then easily believed to inhabit it? So that they were worshipping the stone *as* the stream? Throughout mythology, fairy tales and ballads, changes of form between immortals, humans, animals and inanimate nature are disconcertingly easy. Zeus becomes a bull or a swan, Daphne a tree, Arethusa a fountain, Lot's wife a pillar of salt. Witches turn people to stone—the King's Men at Rollright, for instance. Standing stones go down to running water at midnight for a drink—a habit of the Naked Boy at Sminhays on the Brendons ridge road. In the half-light, or the willing suspension of

48

CARATACUS STONE. This stone on Winsford Hill, thrown down by vandals in 1923, was expertly re-erected, under a shelter, at the wish of Sir Thomas Acland.

In the Middle Ages, as the Langeston, it had been a Forest boundary stone. The Dark Ages inscription is on the uphill side—perhaps implying that the ancient track ran nearer the ridge than today's road. Possibly the stone was first a mark of stream-worship in the Bronze Age.

49

disbelief, might not the Challacombe Longstone be a tall old man stooping towards his stream, and Anstey a veiled lady presiding over hers?

★

That is speculation. But summarising, what can we reasonably infer from the barrows and stones about the people who set them up with such care?

Certainly they believed in an after-life. The food and drinking cups in the early graves would provide sustenance for a short journey. The Bampfylde necklace may have been buried as a reminder of the mourners, or as a mark of distinction to be worn in another world, or, like a wedding ring today, to ensure that what the dead person treasured should never belong to anyone else.

Clearly it was thought right that the great should be remembered with honour. The Bronze Age Greeks buried Achilles, who had died a long way from home, in a fine barrow on a foreland, so that sailors far out at sea would recall him to mind. Their contemporaries here chose commanding sites on the ridges, near to the chieftain's own people and seen from afar by strangers travelling overland.

Some of these high places seem to have been sanctified by religious observances; perhaps burial there ensured the special protection of the gods. It looks as if the sun and certain streams were considered divine, and in three places, Chapman Barrows, Five Barrows and Withypool Hill, the concentration of stone monuments and barrows in significant relationship to sun or stream-head, or both, hints at a belief that their life-giving power would reach into the grave. Culbone Row, running from a barrow to an eastern hill top, seems to tell the same tale.

But nobody yet understands the little stone settings; and indeed they may prove to be secular, not religious at all.

4   *Everyday Life*

Inevitably one asks where the builders of these earth and stone monuments lived. And how did they live? Who travelled the ridgeways, and why?

Exmoor may have been more thickly populated in the second millennium BC than ever before or since. Earlier, the Mesolithic people were probably nomads, and the Neolithic perhaps only summer visitors. The Bronze Age families or tribes enjoyed the hill sunshine for about a thousand years before the worsening climate drove them down to the foothills. When the Iron Age invasions grew serious, the uplands may have become a place of uneasy refuge, while successive newcomers farmed the lower fringes. Any traces of a settled life on the high ground are likeliest to date from the Bronze Age.

But we know pitifully little about the everyday life of these hillmen. The enquiry is much further forward in Wiltshire and on Dartmoor. Here it has only lately begun to be more than haphazard, and this chapter should be written ten or fifteen years hence, not now. At present it has to be an almost empty chart, with a few shoals and promising channels lightly pencilled in.

First the shoals. A serious problem in trying to decipher the ground evidence is the dating. The moor has been used for much the same purposes—farming and occasionally a little mining—for 4000 years. In the long cold wet winters a sunny leeward slope must always have been a boon. A shepherd's cot built of simple materials and thatched is soon destroyed by the weather if it is abandoned, so a ruin may look much older than it is. Local memory lasts a few generations, but the old sheep farmers seldom kept records, and nobody really knows when or how long these humble little dwellings stood.

Old field banks on the open moor are equally difficult. Inside the Forest they are almost bound to be pre-Norman or post-1820, but outside it one commoner might, by agreement with the others, enclose a small patch and till it for a few years before letting it revert, exhausted, to heather. This custom, on record in the 17th century, may already have been hundreds of years old. In winter sunlight, ridges can be seen on Withypool and Molland Commons, and long banks, not much worn down, on Braddymoor and on Middle Hill. All these are likely to be mediaeval or later. It now seems possible to distinguish prehistoric field walls too, but the difference needs a practised eye.

Other low earth and stone banks form rings and approximate rectangles. These simple shapes suit so many purposes that they may date from almost any period. Anything circular, for instance, suggests the Bronze Age people, who evidently liked the shape, and used it for religious and ceremonial sites and for their houses—as at Grimspound on Dartmoor. There is, of course, great aesthetic pleasure in a circle—and no reason why they should not have felt it. It has universal appeal as the perfect form, having, like eternity, neither beginning nor end. A round enclosure is good for some ceremonies, or for watching any kind of performance, or for conference between equals. It may also have been easier to build, in early days, than a rectangle, which looks badly wrong unless the corners are exactly right.

But a circle did not cease to be a useful shape when the Bronze Age ended. 'Round houses' are not yet obsolete. Toll gates were not required on Exmoor, but treadmills worked by horses were usual on hill farms within living memory. And in the 19th century the new owners of the Forest, John Knight and his son, brought down Scottish shepherds, who introduced the northern stells. These were wall banks planted with trees, making a sheltered ring where the sheep were safe in the worst snowstorms. There is a beautiful one, a dome of beeches, at Three Combes Foot.

So conundrums abound. A grassy embanked ring inside the Forest wall, near Gammon's Corner where there was a telling-house, is often called a stell, but it has no trees. It would be a good place for a pound, since it is near an old track leading out of the Forest, and sheep could be gathered there before being counted out, but it has no entrance. On the saddle between Badgworthy Hill and Hoccombe Hill are two rings about a hundred paces apart. They are 25 and 15 paces across and have entrances E and SSE respectively, the former looking as if it had been a neatly revetted gateway. Their stone walls or banks, not more than 2ft high now, are grassed over, and they have no trees. They are within easy distance of a few round barrows, two stone settings, and the mediaeval long-houses which, as 'the land of the hermits of Bagawordia' were given to the Brethren of the Hospital of Jerusalem in the twelfth century. (These are the 'Doones' houses' of Blackmore's romance). In the other direction, not far away, are a few banks in the heather and a small rectangular ruin which a shepherd might have built not very long ago. Close to the second ring is a shell hole from gunnery practice in the second world war. It is really very difficult.

Rectangles are not much easier. Neolithic people and Roman colonists used them for building, and so, later on, did Saxons and Normans. Mediaeval long-houses are adjacent squares, more or less. But walled fields of any age may be roughly rectangular, and the shape remained useful not only for cottages and farm buildings but for pens and sheep dips out on the moor, right on through mediaeval times to our own day.

52

19th century mining raised earthworks too. A site on Hangley Cleave, near Two Barrows, shows what a maze of pits and hillocks might remain. Or sometimes a single attempt left a small neat ruin. A shaft filled in and capped, within the high ring of earth cast up when it was dug, can look like a bowl barrow with a deep cup hollowed out of its centre. This may account for a ring on Almsworthy Common, near Chetsford Water, which stands, perhaps fraudulently, near a great many Bronze Age relics.

One more shoal needs care. How primitive were the people who lived on Exmoor in the second millennium BC? Ground evidence, and comparison with other uplands, may eventually answer this, but what is seen on the ground depends partly on what the observer is looking out for. We may have too few categories. Preconceptions may be blinkers. Should we, for instance, still be talking about hut circles? Archaeologists studying the Dartmoor settlements have dropped the term as too disparaging, and speak of 'round houses', to show that they do not mean hovels.

Lately, while anthropologists have been seeking parallels among people who still live in pre-technological conditions, astronomers have shown that Stonehenge was not only a temple to the sun-god but also an astronomical observatory, perhaps the first ever built. A distinguished engineering scientist, after much measuring, infers that though the Bronze Age people of Britain could neither read nor write, they were phenomenally good calculators, arranging timber and stones in complicated geometrical patterns related to the planets and the stars. Archaeologists are not invariably convinced by his evidence, and there are other and simpler hypotheses. But the range of conjecture is certainly wide.

On Exmoor, some country thinking may be appropriate. If the peak of the Bronze Age was about three and a half thousand years ago, it is only 140 generations away. Genetically, that is not a lot. Most of us know five generations of one family before we die. Brain power is unlikely to have altered very much in that time, though there was less knowledge available. These people were no fools. They farmed and hunted, probably fished the sea as well as the rivers, and may have found metal locally and worked it. Some of them made long journeys by land or sea. Bird song and the arrival of the swallows, long days, ripe fruit, leaf fall and the stags belling in October would mark the round of the seasons. Time could be measured, and plans made, by the phases of the moon. Countrymen and sailors would have a working knowledge of the night sky without needing to refer to the specialists at Stonehenge.

We know their Greek contemporaries better, from the Odyssey. Homer was writing three or four centuries after Bronze Age Greece had been overrun by Iron Age Dorians, but he came from Ionia, which had

The Buttery Stone.

escaped invasion. He was describing an older way of life from lays carefully memorised and repeated by successive minstrels. The background of his tale is a life of ploughing and herding, of making stone walls on hill farms, of sea-faring and coastal raids, hospitality to strangers, princely gifts of bronze or gold workmanship, and always careful attention to the unpredictable gods, who had to be gratified by tasty sacrifices at every important move. The lord Odysseus built his own boat with a bronze axe. The lord Alcinous entertained him with sports—racing, wrestling and weight throwing, in which all competed—and then a display of excellent dancing, a few young men performing in a cleared ring while others stood round beating time, 'till the air was filled with sound'. The Ithacans assembled at an open-air meeting-place to debate public affairs . . . The customs which Homer took for granted may not have been immensely different from what went on here, and they may hint at other secular structures we should be looking out for, as well as houses, field walls, and roads.

★

The question where so many people lived, during a thousand years or more, when lives were short and generations perhaps four or five a century, depends on another, also unanswered at present—what their homes were made of. On Dartmoor, where clusters of stone houses have long been known by their circular wall-footings, archaeologists are now, during excavation, coming upon traces of wooden ones too. Exmoor, less exposed than Dartmoor and Cornwall, probably had more good timber and certainly not so much hard stone; there may be innumerable rings of post-holes under the peat, on the lower ridges and their flanks. Higher up, stone foundations supporting stakes and wattle may have been customary, or very low walls and a big roof, like a bell tent. Perhaps houses were rebuilt or replaced in nearly every generation, if wood had rotted or soft sandstone crumbled. It is all surmise.

At the beginning of this century, search for ruins of the Dartmoor type led to a great many isolated 'hut circles' being marked on the Ordnance Survey maps, but most of these are now thought to be the retaining rings of bowl barrows, just as the *dolmens* ('stone-tables') of Cornwall and Wales are the uprights with huge roof-stones surviving from long barrows after 4000 years in the wind and the rain. Others may be ring cairns. Some are on slopes which seem too steep for comfortable habitation, though old levelling may be hidden under later tumbled stone. Some are a long way from other known evidence of Bronze Age activity, but fresh discovery may alter that any day.

New traces of probable houses have been found lately, but they are not certainties yet. Some are in sociable groups, some scattered singly among small fields. A very promising cluster in Long Chains Combe was found, quite by chance, on a fine spring day in 1980, by Arthur Phillips, then Warden of the Field Studies Centre at Pinkery. There seem to be between eight and twelve small round houses, with lengths of low wall running from them, some along the contour and some uphill, perhaps separating very small holdings of land. Their position would in Bronze Age weather have been ideal; it is south-facing, high and airy but sheltered, with a sunny little climate of its own as one comes to it round the curve of the hill. A spring rises nearby, and a stream runs below in the combe. The site is rushy and rather remote now, but in its own day it would have had easy access up to Chains Barrow or the saddle at Exe Head, to an enigmatic stone setting on the side of Chains Valley, locally called Short Chains Combe, and down Hoar Oak Water to the settings and rings on Furzehill Common and Cheriton Ridge.

About a mile to the north-west over the hill, at the head of Ruckham Combe, other rings of various sizes are variously interpreted. They lie on either side of the Forest and county boundary, defined here by lesser meare-stones. Two circles north of it are on the maps; two others, just south of it, 40 paces apart, 10 and 8 in diameter, are like a smaller version of the pair on Badgworthy Hill. Slightly further south, on a dry patch of short green grass among the tawny molinia and rush, facing westward, are four small stone rings and a winding bank or ditch side. The position would be just right for young people moving away from Long Chains Combe to new pastures but staying comfortably near their parents and friends. When professional investigation of the Long Chains site becomes possible, some study of this second group might show an interesting link.

Another strange cluster of rings recently recorded is on a north-facing slope on South Common, Parracombe, between Woolhanger and Roe Barrow, across the valley from the probable henge. Again there are two embanked enclosures, one considerably bigger than the other, but in proportion to their size they are closer together. The larger, not circular, and seemingly built of small stones, has a clear entrance, and contains a smaller ring which might be a house within a palisaded garth for stock. The second is less distinct, having been ploughed, and is different in having a number of big boulders in, on, or near its wall; within the ring, off-centre, is a good broadstone, a rectangle 5 ft. by 3 ft., which looks like a fallen upright. Uphill from the two big rings is a smaller one, comparable with the presumed house inside the largest of the group.

Very old wall banks which appear to surround prehistoric fields have been identified during the last few years, either by the interpretation of air photographs or by chance observation on the ground. Those which Corney noticed on Honeycombe Hill are confirmed by the photographs, and others, across the valley on Great Hill, have house foundations among them. Some, worn very low, enclosing a large 'field' with a few small standing stones aligned like sub-dividers within it, were found quite accidentally on Ilkerton Ridge in 1981, and equally by chance, in the previous year, an elaborate field system had been noticed very near to the big stone setting on Almsworthy Common.

On a slight spur between that and Alderman's Barrow a circular wall bank with a southerly gap has been tentatively classified as a large Bronze Age house, but it might belong to a new category. It is visible from east and west on its rise, and exposed to all winds. The position would be much pleasanter for a tribal gathering in summer than for a home in winter. Another suggestion, not very different, is that it might be a small henge. It is also rather like the two rings on the saddle of Badgworthy Hill. And being close to a green road off the Forest, it might have something to do with droving. The wide-open doubt shows the need for scientific investigation. Field work cannot go all the way.

Other houses probably stood at some time in the small enclosures which survive on the slopes or spurs of hills, and these imply stock farming rather than cultivation—protection at night for the small flock or herd. They have a single rampart, likely to have carried a wooden fence, and most are on the lower edges of the moor. They are not heavily defended, and their age is unknown. The design may be old, and the larger of the Woolhanger rings an early example. Some may have been made by late Bronze Age people who had moved down to wooded slopes, where wolves or thieves might lurk. Or they may have been a refuge from marauding invaders. Or Iron Age farmers may have built or adapted them during inter-tribal warfare. And if they were on very good sites they may have been used yet again by the Saxons. It is a question to ponder at Sweetworthy, near Cloutsham, or at Voley near Parracombe, either of which should have provided a pleasant and peaceful farm life. A great many more hill slope enclosures have recently been located from air photographs, and are being checked on the ground. There has been no exploratory excavation at all.

★

Friends and relations visiting each other might use either short local paths or stretches of one of the long highways—literally high ways, staying above the combe-heads, not going down and up again if that could be avoided. These would be trodden tracks, not very precise except where descent was inevitable and a few stones improved a ford, or a tree trunk was thrown across a stream as clammer.

Two of the three long east-west ridges, the northern and the southern, still carry useful roads. The middle one, from Chapman Barrows along the Chains, and perhaps via Rexy to Alderman's Barrow, Bendels and Dunkery, is difficult to envisage as a road now that the Chains are so boggy, but in drier times it might have led to the flat coast beyond Minehead. Possibly the 'preyway' or driftway of Forest times, south of Prayway Head above Simonsbath, had been a branch of the Harepath, and another important track may have left that near Exford to run south-west, skirting Ernesbarrow (near Chibbet Post) and crossing Winsford Hill past the Wambarrows and the Caratacus Stone. West of the moor, it looks as if a road from Combe Martin over Kentisbury, where flints were knapped, linked with the central ridgeway somewhere near Blackmoor Gate and then ran south across Bratton to Mockham Down.

To cross from the southern to the central ridgeway would be easy between Moles Chamber and Woodbarrow, dipping along the undulating course of the later South Molton-Lynton road, or from Kinsford Cross via Blue Gate, unless the Barle was in flood. From the Chains to the coastal ridge would be still easier, either along one of the northern spurs or from Alderman's Barrow past Lucott Cross, Porlock Stone Circle and Hawkcombe Head. Perhaps an old track here determined the Forest boundary after Magna Carta.

There would be no need for elaborate sighting. As Charles Whybrow once trenchantly remarked, the travellers were not explorers. Local people would guide strangers until they knew their way. Most of them would be traders or bronze-smiths—more simply pedlars or tinkers—calling at hillside farms or hamlets as they passed. The ridgeways were easy to follow, running a little below the crest, mostly on the sunnier side, and just above the spring-line. Later, they were used as drove roads for hundreds of years, and parts of them can still be seen alongside the modern tarmac, the barrows testifying to their great antiquity.

Bronze Age people had come here from beyond Sedgemoor, by ways which would be remembered. They must have spread out, as numbers grew, until there was, as now, a network of cousinship all over the moor. They would depend on each other when a job needed many hands, and would share skills as specialisation developed. After a time, curiosity about the distant Dartmoor and Bodmin hills, and Lundy and Wales just across the water, would become irresistibly strong. In all those places, other Bronze Age people were living where Neolithic builders

58

Three-cornered Longstone, Beaple's Hill; from the west.

had left their mark. Certainly there was long distance travel across Exmoor, and barter of some kind, by the middle of the Bronze Age. That amber bead in the grave on Bampfylde Hill had come a long way.

Cornish stone or tin might be on its way eastward, and perhaps Exmoor copper was traded back or forth. There may have been seasonal fairs at henges or stone circles along the route, with religious ceremonies, and feasts in autumn after the slaughter of stock which could not be over-wintered. It may or may not be chance that the Porlock and Withypool stone circles and the Woolhanger henge stand near the three main east-west ridgeways, one by each.

Some people think the Cornish greenstone axes, and perhaps the tin, were taken eastward by sea—either up the English Channel to Poole, or along the north coast of the peninsula to the Severn estuary. But much of this coast is very grim indeed. The high wall of cliffs near Tintagel faces full west, and great Atlantic breakers, swept in by the prevailing winds, crash on enormous crags and pull back with terrible strength. Between Morwenstow and Hartland the wicked rames—long parallel ridges of jagged rock—run out westward into the sea, and grip the wrecks of many centuries in their jaws. From Morte Point to Minehead there are very few easy havens, and the rise and fall of the tides is among the highest in the world. Some 150 miles of this, in small open boats, would be an extremely hazardous journey, not to be undertaken with a valuable cargo if there was an easier way overland.

I think there was, and a very important one. South of Exmoor a long ridge road runs from SW to NE, between Chulmleigh and Dulverton. Eastward its line would cross the Barle and the Exe just above their confluence, and the Haddeo at Bury, and go on over Haddon Hill to join the Harepath at Elworthy Barrows. South-westward, the ridge road passes big round barrows, and for fifteen miles points straight towards the Cornish hills before dropping to the Taw at Eggesford. Holding that direction would take it past Hatherleigh and over Broadbury (Bronze Age and Roman), north of Launceston and then across Bodmin Moor as though pioneering the A30, past Bronze Age Altarnun, Roman Nanstallon, Castle-an-Dinas, strongly fortified in the Iron Age, Carn Brea (Neolithic, Bronze and Iron) in the Camborne tin area, and so to St. Michael's Mount, which was known to prehistoric traders from the eastern Mediterranean.

North-eastward from Elworthy Barrows a long-recognised route crosses the Quantocks at the Triscombe Stone, drops down past the mediaeval castle to Nether Stowey, past Cannington, a hill occupied in the Dark Ages, and so to the Parrett estuary at Combwich, a little river port in Roman times and now. If the way then became amphibian, either by ferry to a footpath along the rim of land between Sedgemoor and Severn or by broad shallow coastal boats right up to the Bristol Avon, it would give an approach by water up the Axe to the Mendip lead, which was used before the Romans came, up the Brue to the Lake Villages where Iron Age craftsmen worked in bronze, and up the Avon to Bath and the southern tip of the Jurassic Way, which is a well-attested prehistoric road to the mouth of the Humber and perhaps the Baltic trade.

The way towards and through Cornwall, passing near places which were once very important, is not proved. Close work at a few fords or cross-roads might confirm it. Meanwhile, at this end several scraps cohere.

Long ago an Exmoor farmer who had grown up in the Quantocks told me he thought a track from his farm near Withypool must once have led to Combwich, 'where King Arthur took his troops across'. A mile and a half inland from Combwich is the low hill of Cannington, where traces of late Romano-British occupation, including sherds of pottery of Lake Village type, were found during excavation. Malory's tale of Sir Gareth begins when King Arthur held the high feast of Pentecost 'at a city and a castle, in those days that was called Kynke Kenadonne, upon the sands that marched nigh Wales'.* It ends with the marriage celebrations which the king, Gareth's uncle, recommended should be held 'at Kyng Kenadowne by the seaside, for there is a plenteous country'. Dame Lyonesse had been besieged in the Castle Perilous beside the Isle of Avylon (Glastonbury) which could be reached by land or sea, and her brother Sir Gryngamour took her to 'Kyng Kenadowne' for her wedding. Was it Cannington, passing into legend like Nestor's palace at sandy Pylos?

A little way south-west of Knowstone Inner Moor and its two Bronze Age barrows the road forks at Beaple's Hill. The main ridge goes on towards Cornwall, but a spur-road runs westward through Rose Ash and across Munson farm before twisting away downhill, and it was known until lately, by people living near it, as Rattle Street (*Street* as in Watling Street; it runs through open country). The Glastonbury-type bowl unearthed at Munson closely resembled one found in North Cornwall. Both were dated to the years just before the Roman conquest.

At the old road fork stands a shoulder-high column of conglomerate stone. Its lower half is smoothly cylindrical. Part of the upper half, on the north side, has flaked off, leaving three blunt weathered corners pointing east, west and south. Southward, an old hedge-line shows that the modern road has deviated. The stone is very cleverly placed, as the concrete triangulation post 200 yards to the west makes clear. From the south-west road and from Rattle Street one sees the concrete stump but *not* the longstone; the two roads converged, and an eastbound traveller on either would be in no doubt of his way. But anybody coming from the north-east would need a sign at the fork, and he had the longstone on the skyline ahead of him for at least a mile. The concrete post on the true summit does not appear from the NE, though the difference in altitude is minute.

The age of the longstone is a mystery, because of the smoothly-shaped lower half. The barrows show that the route was in use in the Bronze Age. The fork was where an Iron Age trader from the Lake Villages would turn west to Munson or keep on south-west for Cornwall.

* Name spelt in two ways, according to Vinaver's edition of the Winchester MS, a better text than Caxton's.

Perhaps when a long series of wooden posts had rotted away a stone was brought up for permanence—a broken column, for instance, which somebody thought would meet the need?*

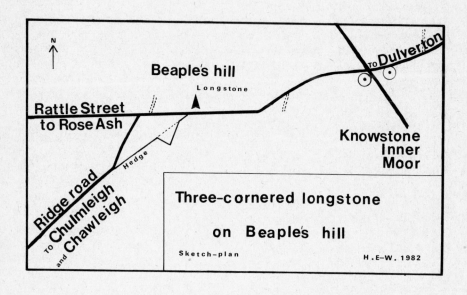

Beaple's hill

Longstone

Rattle Street
to Rose Ash

Ridge road
to Chulmleigh
and Chawleigh

Hedge

to Dulverton

Knowstone
Inner
Moor

Three-cornered longstone

on Beaple's hill

Sketch-plan

H.E-W. 1982

*The proposed motorway from Tiverton to Barnstaple is likely to pass very near the stone, and may make the relationship difficult to see. Two broad and clumsy grooves make a long V in the lower half, on the NE side, like a rough re-emphasis of the directions. The modern contribution is a neat bench-mark on the southern curve.

The slab lying at the foot is of different stone, probably placed there quite recently to be out of the ploughman's way.

5　War and Change

On various hill tops round the edges of the moor are prehistoric 'castles'—
Shoulsbury looking down to the Taw estuary, several Bury and Berry
castles (*bury* is *burg* and *borough,* and seems to have meant first a fortified
enclosure), Mounsey and Brewer's and Oldberry castles all on the Barle
just above Dulverton, and others near the coast. Young visitors hoping
for battlements and dungeons are sadly disappointed to see only earth
and stone banks of no great height, almost covered with grass, surrounding an uneven stretch of rough pasture. It might be better to think of
sand castles on the beach standing against the incoming tide.

Unlike the hillside enclosures, these hill-top forts are quite obviously
designed to resist human attack. Not one is securely dated, but the earliest
were probably built by Bronze Age people against the warriors with
iron weapons who had crossed from Gaul, and many of the later ones
by these invaders fighting each other, before the Roman conquest
imposed peace. Nearly four hundred years later, when the legions were
recalled and the Romanised Britons had to fend for themselves, some of
the old 'castles' may have been renovated and used again.

The only defence works yet excavated are the two Roman fortlets on
the northern cliffs, Old Burrow and Martinhoe, which were used for a
short time very soon after the Claudian invasion of 43 AD as look-out
posts against the unconquered tribes in South Wales. No other sure
signs of Roman occupation are known on Exmoor, where the hill
farmers were probably giving no trouble as long as they were left alone.
It is not clear how the handful of soldiers at the little forts had come from
Exeter, nor how they were supplied, but the whole episode lasted less
than thirty years—two at Old Burrow, then about twenty at its more
convenient successor, Martinhoe. When the need ended, the profes-
sionals went away.

Tentative dating of the hill forts depends on study of their structure,
comparison with those excavated elsewhere, and an attempt to understand their siting. Charles Whybrow's careful work on all this was
published in the *Proceedings of the Devon Archaeological Society* No. 25 (1967).
In *Antiquary's Exmoor* he explains the characteristics from which dates
are inferred. The main differences lie in the type of rampart and the
form of gateway.

The Exmoor ramparts are not nearly as complex as those of the big
Iron Age forts further east, such as Maiden Castle where the fighting
between Romans and Belgae was deadly serious. The simplest are the
single wall banks, more or less circular, with an outer ditch and a

Cow Castle.

causeway across it to the entrance, and doubtless a barricade along the top of the wall. These seem to have been the earliest, built by Bronze Age people to protect themselves and their stock. Beacon Castle on the Martinhoe/Parracombe boundary, Roborough near Lynton, Gallox Hill near Dunster, probably date from this time.

Later, when the newcomers were attacking each other and stronger defences were needed, close attention was paid to the choice of site. If the spur of a hill was forbiddingly steep on two or three sides, outer ramparts need not be built except at the easiest approach. The contour was used in this way at Myrtlebury near Lynton, and at Berry Castle on the Luccombe/Porlock boundary, and also, of course, at the promontory fort of Hillsborough at Ilfracombe.

The early gateways were too easy to force. The next device was to build the ends of the rampart overlapping, so that an intruder would have to turn left, exposing his unprotected sword arm to the enemy. More elaborate again was the entrance between inward-turning ramparts—as at Hillsborough and Elworthy—so that the defenders posted on the ends could concentrate on the men rushing in to storm the gate, while those on the main wall attended to the attackers still outside. (A Roman variant on this plan appeared at Old Burrow. There, a rough circular outer rampart surrounded an open space with a sturdy square fort in the middle of it. Outer and inner entrances were on opposite sides, so that any tribesmen who had fought their way into the enclosure had to run half way round the real fort, as though in a trap, to reach its well-defended gate).

The evidence of technical development in fort building confirms what Romans said about the British Gauls—that they were bellicose people, much given to tribal warfare. It tells us very little else. This is how the defences were planned, but how much were they used? And why? Who was fighting whom? Were the hill forts refuges, or bases for mutual cattle raiding, or were they designed for serious war?

Their size and position may sometimes be indicative. Most of them are small, and most are on the fringes of the high ground. A few are perched above rivers, and a few command the ends of long ridges. Cow Castle, where White Water joins the river Barle below Simonsbath, seems more like a refuge than a power base. Perhaps the tribe retreated there with its livestock until armed strangers following the stream, or passing along the Harepath a mile to the north, were safely out of the way.

Mounsey Castle, in a loop of the Barle above Dulverton, would serve such a purpose still better. It stands on the crest of a thickly wooded hill, and spreads pear-shaped from a narrow rocky ridge outside the north gate. Westward, the hill drops away sharply to the river far below, and it is only a little less steep on the south and east. Within the big rampart, on what is now a clearing among tall trees, a wide terrace surrounds the upper level, the real retreat. The southward entrance has one side turned inward and the other outward. If the gap was barred by felled tree trunks, the attackers would have a very difficult task.

The river itself would check besiegers, and unless the whole hill was surrounded would provide water on one side or the other for the occupants. Hills to the north are higher, but safely out of bowshot; and it was interesting to notice, on a sunny April afternoon in 1982, when the beech buds had not unfolded, and although several big trees had been uprooted by winter gales, that the large clearing could not be seen from these hills. The domes of bare trees appeared to cover the whole summit. It recalled Caesar's note that 'the Britons apply the term "strongholds" to densely wooded spots fortified with a rampart and trench, to which they retire in order to escape the attacks of invaders'. There seems no reason why hostile tribes pushing upstream should even know the hill fort was there; and if they did, a scout sent uphill to reconnoitre might well advise his friends not to attack.

An alternative theory is that the camp protected a ford crossed by a north-south road, but though there are mediaeval boundaries along the Barle and the Danesbrook just here, and others by lanes from Five Cross Ways to the south through Oldways End, the existence of any prehistoric track is less sure. (The name *Oldways End* is recent, and a snare; the local pronunciation, *Allways End*, fits the facts better). Another question is whether these Iron Age tribesmen would have built so carefully to protect anybody except themselves, unless the reason for an alliance was very strong. It is hard, now, to see such a reason at Mounsey.

The castles standing where long ridge roads leave the moor may be a different matter. Three are notable—Shoulsbury Castle, Mockham Down Camp, and Elworthy 'barrows'. All three are unusually big for Exmoor, and each is on a broad plateau. Shoulsbury, at 1500 ft., looks westward over foothills to the navigable Taw estuary and far out to sea, and northward to Holdstone and Trentishoe on the Channel coast. Mockham Down, at 1000 ft., stands at the end of the southward road from Kentisbury over Bratton Down, and looks to Dartmoor, to Lundy, and back to Five Barrows. The unfinished *bury* of Elworthy, at 1250 ft., has the immense Brendons view, to Wales and up the estuary of the Severn past Mendip, to the Quantocks and across southern Sedgemoor as far as the foot of Salisbury Plain, and southward to the Blackdown Hills. From each of these three, defenders might see an enemy far off, and prevent his gaining a foothold on the high tracks across the moor. The hill tribes may have thought it worth combining their strength against a common foe.

The attempt at alliance cannot have been very successful. Shoulsbury may be incomplete. Elworthy certainly is—one section of it was never started. Charles Whybrow thought it might have been begun in a hurry, shortly before the Roman invasion, when some of the powerful Belgae, striking westward, were harrying and burning on Mendip and along the Severn coast. Perhaps the danger ended abruptly. Whatever the reason, the work was left unfinished.

UNDATED HEAD from Combe Farm, West Anstey, 1979.
The farmer, Jeffrey Samuel, found this lump of iron-rich claystone,
5-6 cm. wide, face downward under the turf in a patch of old pasture,
at the head of a broad combe, where he had previously found prehistoric flints
and mediaeval pottery. The face may have been engraved during the
Dark Ages or it may be a mediaeval grotesque. As yet, nobody knows.

Of these Iron Age people on Exmoor we know only that they built most of the hill-top forts and perhaps some of the enclosed farmsteads on the slopes; that they used some of the older highroads; and that somebody on Crooked Moor, Rose Ash, offered a bronze bowl of Celtic design to a divinity at the head of a stream.

The Romans left even fewer signs of their rule; but why should Mediterranean people, with most of the island at their disposal, choose to live high up among rain clouds from the salty Atlantic? And the only traces of the dark centuries when the empire had collapsed are the three incised stones—Cavudus which has been moved from the original position which might have explained it, Caratacus which may be a sixth or seventh century memorial cut into a Bronze Age stream-head stone, and at Culbone the wheeled cross carved, aslant, on a slab likely to have been taken from the prehistoric stone row nearby. Along the north coast a few dedications support the tradition that Irish and Welsh missionaries came in by sea, and each holy man with his group of converts built a tiny church. Probably the little Christian communities lived almost in the shadow of the churches to protect them and be protected by them.* The pagans would have no love for apostates.

★

When the Saxons—Christians now, and after long fighting with the Angles beginning to mature into an English nation—at last reached West Somerset, what sort of people did they find on Exmoor?

How can we know? The Gaullish (Gwalish = Walish = Welsh) settlers had either stayed, or been ousted by fiercer kinsfolk coming westward from defeat. Some had been converted by the Celtic missionaries. But what had become of the Bronze Age moormen? They had not been exterminated—the strain of little dark people still persists. Probably they had retreated, at first, to the boggy hills and winding combes, as in other parts of England they slipped away into forests or fens, where it was easy to dodge a pursuer who did not know the land. And in time they became the pixies of the tales, as the Irish fairies stem from the predecessors of the Irish Celts.

The tales show the pixies in a good light. Who were the tellers? The fugitives would not stay in the wilds for ever; when things had settled down, they would cautiously and gradually return, and begin to work for the new owners of the farms. There would be some inter-marriage. As mothers or as nurses, as herdsmen or smiths, they would tell the conquerors' children stories about clever mischievous little people outwitting the clumsy giants, the big raw-boned red-headed Celts, or sometimes deftly helping them, unobserved. Children would love such tales and ask for them again and again. They would be remembered and repeated from one generation to the next, and thus survive two more conquests, when Britons and then English, in similar circumstances, added their rhymes and stories and disguised history to the common stock. We have been mongrels for a very long time.

So far as is known, the Bronze Age people left no written record in any part of Britain, and up here no formal art, though the siting and the shape of barrows and stones often reveal great sensitivity. Without art, an ancient people is dumb to us. It is only in painting and sculpture, in music if one could know the age of a tune, and in the suppleness of poetry, that one can catch any echo of laughter or fun. The shimmer of life is missing. We have only some tiny but fascinating fossils in old tales and ballads.

* Parishes called *Lan-* before a personal name abound in Cornwall. Lan(d)key east of Barnstaple is Exmoor's nearest. *Lan-* is usually understood as an 'enclosure', especially round a church or monastery, but the Welsh version *llan-,* pronounced rather like Scottish *clan,* may point back to an earlier meaning—the Christian 'family' of the missionary or the converted chief.

Do the pixy stories, half-believed on Exmoor until very lately, contain shreds of great antiquity in their childish charm and pathos? Did the men and women who gathered in the sunshine at henges and circles 'laugh like pixies' at their puckish jokes? They died much younger than we do, but did they enjoy their lives?

We know so little. The Bronze Age people have had, so far, the longest innings since Neolithic times. They farmed and hunted on these slopes, and looked out over these lovely sweeps of hill and sea. They were here until less than a hundred generations ago, and then quietly melted into the landscape. Their tales may be among the first we hear in childhood, but we cannot name one man or woman of them all. On the open moor we can see something of what they did; one day we may understand it.

Naked Boy.

Index of Sites

Note: Sites outside Exmoor are in *italics*.

The Harepath, near Moles Chamber.